THE SURVIVAL GUIDE FOR

TEENAGERS
WITH LD*

*LEARNING DIFFERENCES

THE SURVIVAL GUIDE FOR

TEENAGERS
WITH LD*

*LEARNING DIFFERENCES

BY RHODA CUMMINGS, ED.D.
AND GARY FISHER, PH.D.

EDITED BY PAMELA ESPELAND
ILLUSTRATED BY L.K. HANSON

Free Spirit PUBLISHING

Library of Congress Cataloging-in-Publication Data

Cummings, Rhoda Woods.

The survival guide for teenagers with LD* *(learning differences) / Rhoda Cummings and Gary Fisher : edited by Pamela Espeland : illustrated by L.K. Hanson.

p. cm.

Includes bibliographical references and index.

Summary: Provides information and advice to young people who have different learning styles on such topics as dating, driving, getting a job, and planning for the future.

ISBN 0-915793-51-2

1. Learning disabled teenagers—Juvenile literature. 2. Self-help techniques for teenagers—Juvenile literature. [1. Learning disabilities. 2. Life Skills 3. Conduct of life. 4. Self-reliance.] I. Fisher, Gary L. II. Espeland, Pamela, 1951– . III. Hanson, L. K., ill. IV. Title.

HV1569.3.Y3C86 1993   93-6798
362.3'8'0835—dc20   CIP
                                                                        AC

10 9 8 7 6 5 4 3
Printed in the United States of America

Cover and book design by MacLean & Tuminelly

"Eight Tips for Talking to Teachers" on pages 23–24 is adapted from the article, "Ten Tips for Talking to Teachers," from *Free Spirit: News & Views on Growing Up Gifted*, Vol. 2, No. 1, September-October 1988. Used with permission of Free Spirit Publishing Inc.

Free Spirit Publishing Inc.
400 First Avenue North, Suite 616
Minneapolis, MN 55401
(612) 338-2068

Dedication

To Rhoda's children, Courtney and Carter, and Gary's wife, Debbie.

Acknowledgments

Thanks to the folks at Free Spirit Publishing who all work so hard to make these books special. We especially thank Judy Galbraith for having faith in us, and Pamela Espeland for making magic with our words and for being sensitive to the spirit in which the books are written. We want to express our appreciation to John Hirschel and Arlene Morton for their suggestions. Thanks also to all of the teachers and parents who have expressed to us their delight with our Survival Guides. Very special thanks to all the kids with LD who send us letters from all across North America. We love each and every one of you!

About the Authors

Rhoda Cummings studied special education in college; today she teaches it to students at the University of Nevada in Reno. Formerly she taught English and social studies to seventh graders. Rhoda has an adult son named Carter who has LD. Carter lives in Reno, has his own apartment, drives his own car, and has a full-time job. Rhoda has written books for teachers and parents of young people with LD. This is the third book she and Gary have written for young people with LD.

Gary Fisher went to college for many years to study LD, and he has written about it often. Most importantly, he has worked with over 1,000 young people with LD. Some of the students know him as Dr. Fisher, their school psychologist. Gary lives in Truckee, California, and teaches at the University of Nevada in Reno. He helps school counselors and school psychologists learn to work with all kinds of young people, including those with LD.

CONTENTS

IMPORTANT

This book has been written especially for teenagers with LD—people like you. It includes much information that is important to you, including information you won't find anywhere else.

What if reading is hard for you? You're not alone. Eighty percent of all young people with LD have trouble reading. Still, the information in this book is too important for you to miss. Following are some suggestions for getting help.

- Ask someone to read it to you. Try your classroom teacher, your special education teacher, a parent, or a friend.

- Ask someone to make a tape recording of this book for you. That way, you can listen to it whenever you like. You can follow along in the book while you listen.

- This book is available on audiocassette directly from the publisher. For more information, write or call:

  Free Spirit Publishing Inc.
  400 First Avenue North, Suite 616
  Minneapolis, MN 55401
  Toll-free telephone: 1-800-735-7323

INTRODUCTION

What LD Means

Some people say that "LD" means "learning disabled" or "learning disabilities." Others say it means "learning different" or "learning differences." When we say LD, we always mean "learning different" or "learning differences" because we believe that each person learns in his or her own way.

Gary remembers, "School was easy for me, but I have never been good at putting things together. For example, once I bought a cart for my microwave. The cart had to be assembled, I had a hard time with it, and I became very frustrated. So I called my friend Eric[*] and asked him to come over and help me. He put the cart together in a flash."

When Gary was in school, he had no trouble learning to read. When Eric was in school, he was called LD and got special help with reading. Gary is terrible at putting things together, but Eric has a talent for it. Who is smarter, Gary or Eric? The answer is: Both are smarter, but in different ways. Both have learning differences.

If you are reading this book, you probably have been identified as a person with LD. Your learning differences may make it difficult for you to learn some school subjects. For example, maybe you have problems with reading but not in math. Or perhaps you have trouble in math but not in reading. Or maybe you can read easily but you can't remember what you read. Some students with LD have trouble with all school subjects.

---

[*] "Eric" is not the real name of Gary's friend. All names of people we know have been changed to protect their privacy.

1

When you aren't in school, you may not notice any difference in the way you learn things. In fact, you may have an easier time learning certain things than some other people.

"Sometimes people ask me, 'Are you stupid or something?' But I'm smart in some things and not so smart in others. I like to cook and I'm good at electronics." Rupert, 15

What LD Doesn't Mean

One thing LD never means is "dumb" or "retarded." Before you were identified as a person with LD, you were tested to find out why you were having trouble with school subjects. One of the tests you took was an intelligence test, and your scores proved that you are not retarded. Retarded means "slow to learn and not able to learn many things," but people with LD *can* learn many things. If you are in LD classes, this also proves that you are not retarded, because the law says that people who are retarded can't be in LD classes.

Another thing LD never means is "lazy." Many people with LD work hard at learning. Of course, it's possible to have LD and still be lazy, but being lazy has nothing to do with having LD.

"When you get your report card and you finally get good grades, someone always says, 'Oh, you're just in special ed.' What is that supposed to mean? That my B isn't as good as theirs?" Megan, 17

Why We Wrote This Book

This is our third book for young people with LD. Our first is called *The Survival Guide for Kids with LD*, written for ages 8 and up. In that book, we emphasize that kids with LD are not alone. There are many young people with LD. During the 1989-1990 school year, over 2 *million* students in the United States took part in educational programs for people with LD.

Our second book is called *The School Survival Guide for Kids with LD: Ways to Make Learning Easier and More Fun*. We wrote it because many young people who read our first book wanted to know how they could do better in school. *The School Survival Guide* gives specific tips and strategies for improving your performance in math, reading, spelling, and other school subjects.

Meanwhile, people were asking, "What about teenagers with LD? When are you going to write something for them?" This book is our response. It's different from our first two books because teenagers have different interests and concerns, such as planning for the future, becoming independent, dating, driving, and getting a job. These are some of the topics we address here.

How to Use This Book

There is no special way to use this book. It isn't a textbook, although you may be reading it in school. If you're reading it on your own, just skim the Contents, pick a chapter that appeals to you, and jump in.* (One suggestion: If you don't know much about LD, we hope you'll start with Chapter 1. You'll get more out of the other chapters if you understand the basics about LD.)

Is there something special you want to read about immediately? Check out the Index. It will point you toward every topic covered in this book.

If after you read *The Survival Guide for Teenagers with LD* you feel like writing us a letter, please do. We love to get letters from our readers, and we answer every letter we receive. Tell us what you think of our book. Let us know how it helps you, or give us some ideas for making it better. Your thoughts and opinions are important to us.

---

* Remember: If reading is hard for you, *get help*. Turn to the page before the introduction for ideas.

Send your letter to us in care of our publisher at the following address:

Rhoda Cummings and Gary Fisher
c/o Free Spirit Publishing Inc.
400 First Avenue North, Suite 616
Minneapolis, MN 55401

Best Wishes,

Rhoda Cummings and Gary Fisher
Spring 1993

UNDERSTANDING LD

Since LD means "learning different," it makes sense that there are different kinds of LD. As we describe each type, think about which one sounds like you.

Five Kinds of LD

1. Academic LD.

People with academic LD may have trouble with school subjects such as English composition, math, social studies, and science. They may have trouble with one subject or more than one. But they are often good at other things like art, music, sports, or mechanics.

Rhoda says, "I once had a student named Teresa who had problems with reading, so she learned by listening or looking at pictures. Teresa had a lot of friends, including boyfriends, and she was a terrific basketball player. She didn't let her reading problems slow her down. She graduated from high school and went on to attend community/junior college—on a basketball scholarship."

2. Language Learning Disability.

People with a language learning disability have good ideas, but they have trouble finding the right words to describe them. They hear the words that other people say, but they don't always understand what the words mean. They might ask people to repeat what they say. If you have a language learning disability, other people may not realize it. They may think you aren't listening and get angry with you or laugh at you when you ask them to repeat something.

A friend of ours named Woody has a language learning disability. One day his history teacher was telling the class about Captain Cook, a famous explorer. When she asked the class to tell what Captain Cook was famous for, Woody said, "He cooked meals for all the sailors." Everyone laughed, including Woody— except he didn't know what he had said that was so funny.

3. Attention Deficit Disorder.

Gary says, "Once I was testing a boy named Maurice who has attention deficit disorder. We were working in a room that was very near to the school office. Every time someone went in or out of the office, Maurice would stop what he was doing to ask, 'What was that?' Finally we moved to a different room where there were no outside noises. Maurice was able to finish the tests without any problem."

Attention deficit disorder (ADD) and LD are not the same, but up to 40 percent of young people with LD may also have ADD. If you have ADD, it may be hard for you to concentrate on your school work, pay attention in class, and block out distractions. For example, when you hear a noise outside the classroom, you may start listening to the noise instead of the teacher's lecture. When someone gets up to sharpen a pencil, you may stop what you are doing and watch that person. Or you may be impulsive, saying or doing things without thinking and getting into trouble as a result.

We all have many thoughts at the same time. Most people without ADD can shut out the "extra" thoughts that aren't important right now. They can concentrate on one thing at a time. If you have ADD, your brain may not be able to shut out the "extras." That's why it's so hard for you to concentrate.

Some students with ADD take medication to make it easier for them to pay attention. Some of the most commonly prescribed drugs are Dexedrine, Ritalin, and Cylert. For students whose ADD makes it difficult or impossible to learn in school, medications can help. However, we believe that many attention problems can be helped without drugs. For example, students with ADD may be moved to a place in the classroom where there are fewer distractions. Or they may ask their special education teacher to show them some ways to handle their impulsive behaviors.

If you are taking medication for ADD, find out more about it. Talk to your parents* and your doctor about the drug. Ask if it has any side effects; some medications can *cause* problems as well as solve problems. Ask if there are other ways besides drugs to deal with your ADD.

4. Perceptual Motor Disability.

Some people with LD have trouble using a pen or pencil, so their handwriting may be hard to read and their work may be messy. They may have to erase and rewrite, leaving big holes in the paper. If you have perceptual motor disability, ask your teacher if you can do your written work on a computer. Then you can correct mistakes without erasing.

Also, people with a perceptual motor disability may not be very good at games and sports that require coordination and quick reflexes.

---

* When we use the word "parents" in this book, we mean any adults who are legally responsible for you until you become legally responsible for yourself at age 18.

5. Social Perceptual Disability.

People use body language to send signals about their feelings and needs. For example, a frown is a signal that means, "I'm unhappy" or "I'm angry." A tapping foot may be saying, "Hurry up. I'm getting impatient."

Some people with LD can't understand these signals. For example, imagine that Bob and Keith are talking about something serious and personal. Suddenly Tom comes up and tries to join the conversation. Bob and Keith stop talking and stare at Tom. Bob frowns, Keith rolls his eyes, sighs, and crosses his arms over his chest. All of these are signals that say, "You're interrupting; go away." But Tom has a social perceptual disability, so he can't read the signals correctly.

Gary says, "Once I took a group of teenagers with LD on a camping trip. A family with two teenage daughters was at the campsite next to ours. Henderson, one of the boys in my group, decided that he wanted to talk to the girls. While the family was eating lunch at a picnic table under a tree, Henderson started throwing rocks at the tree, trying to get the girls' attention. At first the family ignored him, then they glared at him, but Henderson ignored these signals. Finally the parents told him to go away."

What Causes LD?

Nobody really knows for certain what causes LD. Just as there are different kinds of LD, there are probably many different reasons why people have LD.

For example, sometimes LD seems to run in families. You may have a parent, uncle, or cousin with LD. Some people had an accident or illness when they were very young which may have caused their LD. Occasionally, something happens during pregnancy or birth which may result in LD. Some children learn less than others before they start school, so they are behind from the beginning and it's hard for them to catch up. When they start school, these kids fall even farther behind, and they may be identified as having LD.

Some children don't get enough to eat when they are babies, or they don't get enough of the right kinds of foods. Poor nutrition can affect their ability to learn later in life.

Other children may not have any problems with learning until they start school and something interferes with their education. Perhaps one of their parents becomes very ill, which disrupts the family and makes it hard to concentrate on learning. Or maybe their family moves around a lot, never staying in one place long enough to get settled. There may be many reasons why these children fall behind in school. Whatever the reason, they may be identified as having LD. Some of them may really have LD. But others may just be so far behind that it only *seems* that they have LD.

FIVE FACTS ABOUT LD

1. People with LD are found in all countries and cultures in the world, not only in the United States and other English-speaking countries.

2. Nearly half of all school-age children with disabilities have LD.

3. Of all the students identified as having LD, about 72 percent are boys and 28 percent are girls.

4. Most children with LD are identified in elementary school. Few are newly identified in junior high/middle school or high school. (Maybe this is partly because many teenagers with LD drop out of school.)

5. Seventy-eight percent of students with LD receive their education in regular classrooms and resource rooms. Twenty-one percent are in special classes for students with LD.

Getting Into an LD Program

If you're in an LD program, you may be wondering how you got there. Usually, the process works something like this.

At some point in your schooling—probably during elementary school, or perhaps during middle school/junior high or high school—your teachers or parents became concerned about your school performance. You may have been having problems with one subject or many. Your teacher, school counselor, or principal decided that you should take some tests to help determine why you were having problems with your school work. Your parents had to give their permission for you to take the tests. In some schools, you can sign up for the tests yourself at age 16 or 18.

We don't know exactly which tests you were given, but it's likely that they included intelligence tests (also called "aptitude tests") and achievement tests.* Maybe you were asked to put blocks or shapes together to match a picture, or to put pictures in order to tell a story. Someone probably checked your eyes and ears to find out whether you could see and hear adequately. You may have taken additional tests to find out whether you had difficulty understanding or using language.

If you're curious, ask your teachers or parents which tests you took. Some common aptitude tests are:

- the WISC (Wechsler Intelligence Test for Children— ages 5-16),

- the WAIS (Wechsler Intelligence Test for Adults— ages 16 and up),

- the Stanford-Binet Scales of Intelligence, and

- the Kaufman ABC Test of Intelligence.

Some common achievement tests are:

- the WRAT (Wide Range Achievement Test),

- the PPVT (Peabody Picture Vocabulary Test),

- the Key Math Test, and

- the Woodcock Reading Master Test, Test of Written Spelling, and Test of Adolescent Language.

When the tests were completed and scored, your parents attended a meeting at your school, and the people who tested you presented and explained your test results. They told your parents that you had LD, and they recommended that you become part of the LD program at your school or a different school. Next, an Individualized Education Plan (IEP) was written especially for you, describing what you would be working on in the LD program.**

---

* You'll learn more about tests and testing in Chapter 2.
** You'll learn more about the IEP in Chapter 2.

Your IEP is reviewed after six months and rewritten every year you are in the LD program. Every three years, you take the same tests you took at the beginning. Sometimes different tests are added. Rewriting your IEP ensures that the LD program continues to meet your needs, which may change over time. Retaking the tests ensures that you still belong in the LD program. Some students stay in the LD program for several years; others stay in it for a year or two. What's important is to get the education that's right for you.

LD isn't like a cold or the flu. It doesn't just go away, and there isn't a "cure." However, some students with mild LD learn to compensate for their learning differences. They may receive all or most of their education in the regular classroom, even though tests show that they are LD. Other students with LD need special education all day, every day. Most students with LD fall somewhere in between. You should be getting the kind of help that meets your needs, and you should keep getting it for as long as you need it. Making sure this happens is one of the tasks of your IEP team.

What You Can Do

Many students in LD programs think they were placed there because they were flunking school, because they are stupid, or because they did something wrong. Now that you've read these pages, you know the real reasons. If you're in an LD program, it's because tests showed that you were a student with LD, and your teachers and parents believed that the program would help you to learn and do better in school.

If you got into an LD program when you were in elementary school, you probably weren't involved in the decision-making process. Now that you're older, you have the right to get more involved, if you want to. We hope that you will. When you take an active role in decisions about your education, you feel more in control of your life. You have a say in what you learn and how you learn. You develop self-respect and positive self-esteem. Following are some suggestions for you to consider.

- Ask to attend the annual meeting about your IEP.

- When you are tested, ask to see the results and to have them explained to you.

- Ask what kind of LD you have and how the LD program is supposed to help you.

- Do you have your own ideas about how you can learn and do better in school? Share them with your parents and teachers. Your ideas may be included in your IEP.

WHAT STUDENTS ARE SAYING ABOUT LD PROGRAMS

"The teachers help you one-on-one. Because there are fewer students in the class, the teachers have more time to work with you." LaRue, 13

"In the regular classroom, all the teacher does is lecture. If you don't take good notes during the lectures, you fail the tests. In the LD program, you can learn in the way that's best for you. Some students listen and take notes. Some tape record the lectures and listen to them later, when they have more time. Some use laptop computers. If you need the teacher to give you a printed outline of the lecture, that's okay, too. You have a choice." Wanda, 15

"I go to regular classes for English and social studies, and to special ed classes for math and science. Some kids in home-room give me a hard time when I leave to go to special ed classes. I'm used to it. To me, they're all the same—rooms where I go to learn." Frank, 16

THE LAW AND
YOUR RIGHTS

IMPORTANT

In school, you have been learning the "three R's": reading, writing, and arithmetic. This chapter is about another "three R's": rights, responsibilities, and respect.

You have special rights as a student with LD. Knowing and exercising your rights can help you to get the education that's best for you. Along with rights come responsibilities—to know your rights; to use them or lose them; and to speak out if you believe that someone is violating your rights. People are more likely to listen when you treat them with respect.

If you are getting special education help in your school because you have LD, then you also have some special rights. These rights are guaranteed by the Individuals with Disabilities Education Act and other federal and state laws.*

- You have the right to an education that is appropriate for your needs.

- You have the right to any related services that are necessary to help you get your education. These services might include speech therapy, counseling, or the use of a computer during school, if you have trouble writing.

---

* This chapter includes general information about your rights under the law. If you want or need more specific information, contact your state's Department of Education or Learning Disabilities Association.

Your Right to an Education That's Right for You

If you are a teenager with LD, it's important to know your rights so you can make sure that your school program is the best it can be for you. This chapter explains the law and the rights it gives you.

The law says that all students with LD have the right to "free, appropriate public education." It also specifies that students with LD have the right to be educated in a regular classroom with children who don't have learning problems, if that is where they learn best. Some students with LD learn best in a resource room, in a special education classroom, or in a special school for students with LD. The law provides for these students, too.

Sometimes people misinterpret the law to mean that all students with LD belong in the regular classroom. This isn't true. If you are in a regular classroom, but you think you could learn better in a resource room or a special education classroom, you and your parents have the right to ask the school to move you there.

Some teenagers with LD who have trouble learning in the regular classroom don't need to go to the resource room or the special education classroom. They just need some extra help with the regular classroom work. If you are in a regular classroom, or if you think you belong in the regular classroom, you and your parents have the right to ask the classroom teacher to make modifications (changes) in the way lessons are presented and in the class assignments.

For example, let's say that you have a hard time reading the assignments in your social studies textbook. Your parents (or you) may ask your teacher to modify the reading assignments. Your teacher might:

- order a version of the book on audiocassette for you to use,
- tape record a reading of the book for you,
- ask a volunteer to read the book aloud to you, or
- give you a special textbook that contains the same information as the regular textbook, but shortened or condensed and written at an easier reading level.

As another example, let's say that you have trouble taking notes or reading assignments written on the chalkboard. Your parents (or you) may ask the teacher if you can bring a tape recorder to class, or your teacher might give you a handout with the assignments written on it. Or you might ask the teacher for a copy of his or her notes. Remember, you have the right to request modifications like these. You're not asking for special treatment; you're asking for your rights under the law.

You may have other problems in the regular classroom that could be solved by asking the teacher to make modifications. Your special education teacher or resource room teacher will know about ways to modify school work; your classroom teacher might talk to him or her. You and your parents may think of other ways. The important thing to remember is this: If you aren't learning well in the regular classroom, you have the right to ask that modifications be made.

"Why am I in special ed? Because I need the help." Carlos, 12

Your Individualized Education Plan (IEP)

If you are a special education student, a special educational plan has been developed for you. Your Individualized Education Plan (IEP) should be ready at the start of each school year. It describes what you will learn that year and how you will learn it, including every class in which you will need special help.

Your plan is written by you, your parents, and an IEP team at your school. Your team will include:

- your special education teacher,
- any regular classroom teacher in a class where you will need special help,
- a school administrator (such as the principal),
- the school psychologist, and
- other school personnel who work with you (for example, the speech therapist or counselor).

You and your parents have the right to attend your IEP meeting. Federal law says that you must be invited if you are 16 or older, but we think that students of all ages should attend their IEP meetings. Don't wait until you turn 16. Tell your IEP team about the ways you learn best and suggest ways that your teachers can help you learn. Ask the team to include your suggestions in your IEP.

Once your IEP has been written, you and your parents should review it carefully. If you agree with the plan, your parents sign it and it goes into action. If you don't agree with the plan, you have the right to request changes until it says what you think it should say.

If you are 18 or older, you may attend your IEP meeting as a full member of the team, equal to every other member. At that age, it becomes your right to agree with your plan and sign it, or to disagree and request changes until you are satisfied. Ask the team to work with you to change any part that doesn't seem right to you.

The IEP is a serious document that should carefully outline your educational program for the year. Sometimes IEPs are written in a hurry and important things are left out. Even if you don't attend your IEP meeting, you should ask to see your IEP. If there's anything on it you don't agree with—or if you believe that something is missing—tell your teacher and your parents. Explain what you think is wrong with your IEP and how you would like it to be changed.

Your IEP can be modified or changed whenever necessary, at any time during the school year. You don't have to wait until your annual IEP team meeting to request changes.

"I was tired of everyone telling me what to learn, and I was tired of learning the same things every year. This year I went to the IEP meeting. I helped set up the goals and pick my classes. I'm happier now and doing better in school." Justin, 15

EIGHT TIPS FOR TALKING TO TEACHERS

In this chapter and in many other places throughout this book, we encourage you to talk to your teachers and other adults whose decisions affect your education and your life. It is your right and your responsibility to speak up for yourself, to offer your opinions, to ask for changes, and even to disagree when something doesn't seem right to you. However, we realize that this may be difficult for some students to do. Adults can be intimidating, especially when they are in positions of power, and speaking up takes courage. Following are eight tips for talking to teachers (and other adults) that we hope will make it easier for you.

1. ***Make an appointment to meet and talk.*** This shows the teacher that you're serious and that you understand a busy schedule. Be flexible and be on time.

2. ***Think about what you want to say before you go into your meeting.*** Write down your questions, concerns, suggestions, or ideas. Make a list of the items you want to be sure to cover. You may want to copy your list for the teacher so both of you can look at it during your meeting.

3. ***Choose your words carefully.*** For example, instead of saying, "I hate to write history reports," try, "Writing reports is hard for me. Is there some other way I can satisfy this requirement for history class?" Instead of saying, "Lectures are boring," try, "It's hard for me to pay attention during lectures. I get distracted and lose track of what you're saying." If you're not good with words, ask another adult to help you come up with the right words.

4. ***Don't expect the teacher to do all of the work or come up with all of the answers.*** Be ready with suggestions and possible solutions. Write them down and share them with your teacher during your meeting. Chances are your teacher will be very impressed—first, because you took the time to generate ideas, and second, because you'll probably come up with some good ideas that are worth trying.

5. ***Be diplomatic, tactful, and respectful.*** Remember that the purpose of your meeting is conversation, not confrontation. Teachers are more likely to help you if you treat them with respect and speak politely.

6. ***Focus on what you need, not on what you think the teacher is doing wrong.*** For example, instead of saying, "The science book is too hard for me to read. You shouldn't have given it to me," try, "I need a science book that's easier to read." Telling people what they have done wrong puts them on the defensive.

7. **Don't forget to listen.** This may seem obvious, but many students need practice in this important skill. If it will help you to remember what your teacher says during your meeting, take notes. Or bring someone along to take notes for you. Later, that person can give you feedback about the meeting; he or she may have heard something you missed. Or, with your teacher's permission, tape record your meeting to review later.

8. **If your meeting isn't a success, get help from another adult.** Speak with your special education teacher or resource room teacher, a guidance counselor, the school counselor, or another teacher or adult you know and trust. Pick someone who is likely to support you and advocate for you, then try tips 1 through 7 again.

Nine Things to Look for in Your IEP

When you ask to see your IEP, it may seem confusing at first because it may have many parts and big words. It helps if you know what to look for. Following are descriptions and explanations of the most important parts. An IEP should include all or most of these items; the specifics of your IEP will depend on your needs and circumstances.

1. A statement about your present level of educational performance.

For example, let's say that you are in the 9th grade, but you are reading at the 5th grade level. Your present level of educational performance in reading would be stated on your IEP as "5th grade."

Your present level of performance is usually determined by achievement test scores or by class work, such as written assignments and tests. It should be stated for each class in which you need special help or modifications. Ask your teacher to look at your IEP with you, show you what it says about your present level of performance, and explain what the numbers mean. What if you disagree with what your IEP says about your present levels of performance? Tell your teacher and ask to take some more tests. You have the right to see your IEP, to have it explained to you, and to ask for changes to be made.

2. Long-term learning goals.

Your long-term learning goals, also called annual goals, should be written as clear statements. They should spell out specific things you will accomplish by the end of the year. You need to be able to read and understand them thoroughly.

For example, let's say that the IEP team decides that you should learn how to balance a checkbook. Your IEP will include a statement something like this: "[YOUR NAME] will be able to balance a checkbook by the end of the year."

Check to see that the long-term goals included in your IEP are right for you. Maybe you would like more goals written into your IEP. Maybe you believe that you can accomplish some of the goals before the end of the year, but others will take longer than a year. Tell your teacher and ask for a revision of your IEP. The more you agree with your long-term goals, the more you will want to work to achieve them.

3. Short-term learning objectives with measurable goals.

These are like the long-term goals, except that they take less time. Short-term objectives are the small steps you take on the way to achieving your long-term goals. For example, the long-term goal, Learn How to Balance a Checkbook, might include these short-term objectives:

- learn how to record checks in a checkbook, and
- learn how to balance a bank statement.

Measurable goals that go along with these short-term objectives might be:

- "Student will record checks correctly 90 percent of the time over a three-month period. This includes recording the date of the check, the check number, the person or business it was written to, and the amount."
- "Student will get the same balance on the checkbook and the bank statement 85 percent of the time over a three-month period."

Each long-term goal included in your IEP should have several short-term objectives with measurable goals.

4. Any special education help you will need.

You and your parents may believe that you can learn in a regular classroom with special help. That help might come from the regular classroom teacher, or from the special education teacher. For example, maybe you would like to tape record classroom lectures so you can review them later. Or perhaps you think it would help to read written outlines of the lectures ahead of time and follow along in class. These ideas should be written into your IEP.

You have the right to make sure that your teachers follow the instructions in your IEP. For example, if your IEP says, "The science teacher will provide reading materials written at the 5th grade level," then that is what should happen. If it doesn't, try reminding your teacher—respectfully—that this is written in your IEP. For example, you might say, "I really need the special reading materials for science—the ones listed in my IEP. How soon do you think I can get them?" If the teacher still doesn't give you the materials, tell your parents or make an appointment to talk to the principal.

Some teenagers with LD don't know their rights. They just sit in the classroom and feel angry or sorry for themselves because they aren't learning anything. They know they could learn, if only their teacher would make a few changes to help them. Now that you know your rights, we hope you will use them to learn as much as you can while you're in school.

Rhoda says, "I once attended an IEP team meeting for Sam, a 17-year-old with LD. Sam and his mother were at the meeting. Some of the teachers started saying that Sam was lazy and didn't want to work, but I knew better. Sam had a good part-time job after school. His boss liked him very much and described him as one of the best workers he had ever hired. Also, Sam knew he wasn't lazy. He stood up for himself at the IEP meeting and told the teachers how they could change things in the classroom to help him learn. Some of his teachers didn't want to make the changes, but Sam and his mother insisted. Sam's mother wouldn't sign the IEP until the changes were written into it, and she asked that the IEP team meet every three months to make sure the changes were being carried out."

5. Any special services you will need.

These might include speech therapy, transportation, or counseling.

Gary says, "Marietta is a 16-year-old with LD. She has a speech problem and needs to see a speech therapist every day, but she goes to a school where the speech therapist only comes once a week. So Marietta's IEP includes a written statement saying that she will receive speech therapy every day from a therapist who works in another school several blocks away. A school bus comes to get Marietta at 2:00 p.m. every day and takes her to the other school."

The law says that you have the right to special services if you need them. You have the right to as many of those services as you need, for as long as you need them. If you have to go somewhere else to get those services, you have the right to ask the school to provide transportation.

6. A statement describing how much time you will spend in the regular classroom.

The law says that students with LD should be included in the regular classroom as much as possible. If you will be in the regular classroom, your IEP should say exactly how much time you will spend there. It should say how much time you will spend in the other places you go to learn, such as the resource room or the special education classroom. The goal, written in your IEP, should be for you to spend more and more time in the regular classroom, if that is right for you. If you learn best with students who are not LD, you have the right to be educated with them.

7. Reasons why you are not receiving all of your education in the regular classroom.

If some of your learning is taking place in the special education classroom and some in the regular classroom, your IEP should give reasons why. For example, let's say that you go to the special education classroom for math. Your IEP should explain why you can't learn math well in the regular classroom.

8. All of the people who will be responsible for making sure that your educational goals and objectives are carried out.

If you spend part of each day in the special education classroom and part in the regular classroom, your IEP should include the names of both the special education teacher and your regular classroom teachers. All of the teachers you will be working with should receive a copy of your IEP. Each of them is responsible for following the IEP requirements.

9. Goals and objectives for helping you plan for life as an adult.

Your IEP should include specific goals and objectives for helping you to prepare for life after high school. These might cover such areas as getting a job, preparing to live on your own, and taking part in school activities that build life skills. Because these goals and objectives are related to the *transition* between being a student and being an adult, they are called an Individualized Transition Plan (ITP). Your ITP may be a separate document, or it may be part of your IEP.

The law says that all teenagers with LD must have a written ITP by the time they are 16 years old. We believe this should happen as early as elementary school. It's never too soon to start planning for your future success. If you are younger than 16, ask for an ITP to be written for you. Make this request at your next IEP meeting.

IEP SUMMARY

- Your IEP should be in place at the beginning of each school year.

- It is written by a team that includes you, your parents, your regular classroom teachers, the school principal, the special education teacher, the school psychologist, and anyone else who is working with you or who has a special interest in helping you get an appropriate education.

- It includes long-term learning goals and short-term learning objectives with measurable goals.

- It lists and describes any special help and services you will need to get a good education.

- It is your right to have an IEP, to make sure that the information on it is correct, to request modifications and changes, and to see that the goals and objectives are carried out.

What You Should Know about Tests and Testing

If you are in a special education program, you have probably taken many different tests. Some measure your achievement in math, reading, and spelling; some measure your aptitude, or ability to learn; others provide insights into your job interests or vocational skills. Tests can give teachers and parents reliable information about how you are doing in school, as long as they are used in the right way. However, sometimes tests are not used in the right way, and they give incorrect or inaccurate information about you. For this reason, the law has some very specific rules about testing students with LD. Following are the rules you should know.

The person being tested should be able to understand the questions on the test.

For example, if the student does not speak English well, then the test should be given in his or her native language.

Gary says, "Manuel is a friend of ours who has not lived in this country very long. When he first enrolled in school, he had a hard time learning, and his teacher suspected that he might have LD. Manuel was given a lot of tests—in English. His test scores were so low that the school psychologist at first thought Manuel was severely retarded. However, the psychologist knew that Manuel's parents only spoke Spanish. Even though Manuel could speak some English, the psychologist decided to give him the tests again—in Spanish. This time, Manuel's scores showed that he had average intelligence. Although he had LD in reading and spelling, he could work math problems at the same level as other students his age."

For some ESL (English as a Second Language) students, it's hard to know the best time to test or the best language to test in. These students may speak English well enough, but not understand it sufficiently to do well on a test. On the other hand, testing in their native language may not be accurate if they have been learning school subjects in English. These students may need to be tested more than once, over a period of time, before the tests show what they really know.

Tests should measure what they say they measure.

Achievement tests provide information about learning in specific school subjects, like math, reading, and spelling. They do not provide information about intelligence or emotional problems, so they should never be used to determine these things. There are other tests that are designed to do this. Don't let someone label you as having "low intelligence" or being "emotionally disturbed" because you failed to do well on a math or reading achievement test.

Tests should be given by people who have been trained to give them properly.

No one should give you any test that he or she is not trained to give. This is especially important if someone is giving you an intelligence test. Intelligence tests should be given only by a school psychologist or a trained diagnostician or psychometrician—someone who has spent many hours learning how to give intelligence tests. These professionals are the only ones who know how to understand the scores on these tests. Also, you should be given an individual intelligence test instead of a group intelligence test.

It usually takes one to two hours to complete an intelligence test. After the test is over, the person who gave the test should score it and prepare a report explaining what the scores mean. The report should be written clearly so that you and your parents can read it and understand it.

If you or your parents don't agree with your test scores, you should ask for an independent evaluation.

Your parents have the right to make this request. If you are 18 or older, you have the right to do this. You may be tested again, this time by a different person. The IEP team must use information from the independent evaluation when they make decisions about your educational program. Sometimes the school will pay for an independent evaluation, and sometimes your parents will have to pay. However, your parents always have the right to ask the school if it will pay.

Scores from a single test may not be used to decide whether you will receive special education.

You should never be placed in a special education program because of your scores on any one test. It doesn't matter if it's an intelligence test or an achievement test; one test is not enough. In fact, test scores should be used only as guidelines by the IEP team when making decisions about your educational program. The best, most important information about your program should always come from your teachers, your parents, and you. You have the right to ask that your program be based on a lot of different information, not just on test scores. We believe that test scores should be the *least* important factor in decisions about your education.

You should be tested in all areas that might relate to your LD.

For example, if you are having trouble reading, you shouldn't be tested on your reading ability alone. Your eyes should be checked to make sure your vision is okay, and your teachers and parents should be asked for their opinions about your reading problem.

Maybe you have trouble reading because you got behind in elementary school. If this is the case, then a good remedial reading program might help you. Or maybe you have trouble reading because it's hard for you to understand how letters fit together to make words. Or maybe the letters move around when you try to read them, and you might do better by listening to tapes instead of reading books. You have the right to insist that you be given enough tests to identify your specific need or problem.

Special Rights for You and Your Parents

The Individuals with Disabilities Education Act also guarantees some special rights for your parents. If you are 18 or older, these rights belong to you.

The right to examine your school records.

You and your parents have the right to see your school records. The law says that your school must comply with your request "without unnecessary delay"—no longer than 45 calendar days. (Some state laws say that schools must comply sooner than 45 days.)

If you or your parents disagree with something that is written in your school records, you have the right to ask that the information be removed. Or you may ask to include a statement in your records that explains your side of the story.

Some schools seem reluctant to let parents see their children's school records. Or they let them see only part of the records. They may make parents wait several days to see the records. For some parents, this can get frustrating. Your parents may need to be patient. Following are two tips for you to share with them:

- Ask if there is a waiting period before records are made available. If there is, ask how long it is. How many days? School days or calendar days? Make an appointment to see your records at the end of the waiting period, or ask the school to send copies to your home.

- Ask to see everything written in your school record.

The right to an impartial hearing.

If your parents disagree with how your IEP is written, they have the right to request a special hearing before a trained and impartial hearing officer. Your school has 45 calendar days (state laws may vary) to reach an agreement with your parents or set up a hearing. If the hearing officer agrees with the school, your parents may decide to sign the IEP, or they may take the case to the state court. If the hearing officer agrees with your parents, the school has the same right to take the case to court. Fortunately, most parents and schools are able to reach an agreement and very few cases go to court.

The right to confidentiality.

You and your parents have the right to expect that all of your school records, test scores, and any other information about you and your educational program will be kept confidential. In most cases, your school may not let anyone besides school personnel see your records without your parents' permission (or your permission, if you are 18 or older). Before asking permission, your school should first make sure that the person who wants to see your records has a valid reason.

Your school should keep a written list of all people who see your records. Anyone who looks at your records must sign and date the list. The list is included in your file, so you and your parents always know who has been looking at your records.

REMEMBER YOUR RIGHTS

You have the right . . .

. . . to get an education that's appropriate for your needs.

. . . to have a written Individualized Education Plan (IEP).

. . . to have your IEP explained so you can understand it.

. . . to ask questions about your IEP.

. . . to agree or disagree with your IEP.

. . . to request that changes be made to your IEP.

. . . to ask for modifications in the way lessons are presented.

. . . to ask for modifications in class assignments.

. . . to understand test questions.

. . . to be tested by people who know what they're doing.

. . . to agree or disagree with your test scores.

. . . to examine your school records.

. . . to expect that your school records will be kept confidential.

HOW TO ADVOCATE
FOR YOURSELF

Can you remember a time when a friend, a parent, or a teacher stuck up for you when you had a problem with someone? Maybe a teacher kept a bigger kid from bothering you, or your mother or father sided with you in an argument with your brother or sister. It would be great if you could count on this happening all the time. But you can't, especially as you get older, so you need to figure out a way to stick up for yourself and let people know the positive characteristics you have. This is called advocating for yourself.

This chapter describes three ways in which people advocate for themselves. Although the first two ways are used by many people, they don't work very well. The third way can help you to get what you want and need.

Passive Advocacy

Jerome went for a job interview at a fast-food restaurant. When the manager asked him to describe his strengths, Jerome looked at the ground and mumbled something that the manager couldn't hear. When the manager asked him to repeat his answer, Jerome said in a slightly louder voice, "I'm a nice guy." He didn't get the job.

Jerome was too passive in his job interview. People who are passive often speak in a soft voice and look at the floor while they are speaking. They don't say what they really want to say, and sometimes they don't say anything at all. For example, Jerome could have told the manager, "I'm a hard worker, I'll be at work on time, and I'm honest." This would have greatly improved his chances of getting the job.

Passive advocates often feel bad about themselves because they allow other people to take advantage of them. Can you remember times when you were passive? Maybe a store clerk waited on someone else when it was your turn, or perhaps another student put you down and you didn't say anything. Later you may have wished you had acted differently, or you may have imagined what you could have said or done. Unfortunately, wishing and imagining won't get you what you want and need.

Aggressive Advocacy

Evan was a 7th grade special education student who went to LD classes for English and math. One day during social studies, another student started teasing Evan about his reading. Evan swore at the student and slapped him in the face. Evan was suspended for five days and got two weeks of detention.

Aggressive advocates try to get what they want or protect themselves by being loud, angry, or physical. These tactics work, up to a point, and aggressive advocates get what they want more often than passive advocates, often because other people are afraid to argue with them. Aggressive advocates also get into trouble more often than passive advocates.

There are other negative consequences of being aggressive. For example, other people may respond by acting aggressive, and they may be bigger, stronger, or more powerful. Aggressive people may not have many friends, and they may feel angry most of the time.

Assertive Advocacy

There is a way to advocate for yourself that won't leave you feeling bad about yourself or angry. We can't guarantee that it will always work, and we can't promise that it will be easy. However, we do know that being an *assertive* advocate will increase your chances of getting what you want and need without getting in trouble, making other people mad, or letting them take advantage of you. Here's how to be an assertive advocate.

1. Decide what you want to accomplish before you start talking. This is called setting goals. It helps you to figure out what's important to you and what you should spend your time and energy on.

2. Use a medium tone of voice—not too loud, not too soft.

3. Make requests or suggestions, not demands or threats. Say, "I want you to stop teasing me," not "Stop teasing me!" and never "If you don't stop teasing me, you'll be sorry."

4. When you are talking to adults, thank them for listening even if you don't get what you want. Plan to try again another time.

Learning to be an assertive advocate takes practice, just like learning to ride a bike or a skateboard. If you feel stupid or afraid that you won't be any good at it, remember what it was like when you first learned to ride your bike. After a while, being assertive will feel as natural to you as riding your bike.

Practice Being an Assertive Advocate

The most effective type of practice is role playing—pretending to be in a situation in which you need to be assertive. Following are three role plays to practice with a friend or an adult. Afterward, think of other situations you might encounter in real life and practice role playing them.

Problem #1: Too much reading.

You are in a regular science class. You are a slow reader, and the teacher has assigned the class 50 pages to read and 10 study questions to answer by tomorrow. You know that it will take you all night to finish that much reading, and you won't have any time to work on the questions.

Assertive Response: What do you want? What's your goal? It has two parts: First, to get your science teacher to understand how your reading problem affects your homework, and second, to convince your teacher to make adjustments in your homework so you can get it done. Keeping your goal in mind, arrange to talk to your teacher after class or after school. Remember to use a medium voice and to make suggestions, not demands. You might say something like this: "I'm worried about the homework assignment. I read very slowly, and I'm getting help with my reading in a special class. Could you give me a shorter amount of reading and fewer questions?"

Don't ask for more time to do the assignment, unless that's your only choice. Homework piles up fast when you're behind, and when that happens, you fall even farther behind. Try to get today's homework done today.

Problem #2: Bugged.

You're talking with a group of your friends in the hall when one of them starts teasing you for being in LD classes.

Assertive Response: What's your goal? To convince your friend to stop making fun of you for being in LD classes. If you feel yourself getting angry, wait until the feeling goes away. (Take a few deep breaths and count to 10.) When you feel calm again, tell your friend in a medium voice, "It bugs me when you say those things about my LD classes. I take them because I need help, not because I'm stupid. I don't want to be around you when you're making fun of me."

"I go to the LD room in the afternoon. A few of my friends ask, 'Where are you going?' It doesn't bother me. I just tell them." Debbie, 14

Problem #3: Curfew.

Your parents have given you a curfew of 10:00 on weekend nights. You would like to be able to stay out later, and you're angry because you think your parents are treating you like a baby. You always have to go home early, before your friends.

Assertive Response: What's your goal? To persuade your parents to let you stay out later on weekend nights. Start by making a list of reasons why you believe you should be able to stay out later. Next, think about the reasons why your parents want you home by 10:00 and try to come up with responses to their concerns. Then write a plan for staying out later. For example: "You want me to be home by 10:00 on Saturday nights, but my friends usually go to a movie that starts at 9:00 and ends at 11:00. I would like to go to the movie with them and out for a hamburger afterwards. I promise to be home no later than 12:00." Finally, prepare to negotiate. Be ready to give up parts of your plan if necessary.

When you're ready with your plan, ask your parents if you can talk to them. Pick a time when the household tasks are done for the evening and explain your plan. Your parents might say "yes" to the movie but "no" to going out afterward because they want you home by 11:30. Since going out was one of the things you were prepared to negotiate, you may have to give it up. Everybody wins: you because you can stay out later, your parents because you'll be home by 11:30. You may want to ask if you can try your plan for a month, then assess how well it worked.

What if your parents reject your entire plan? You may have to try again in the future. Meanwhile, avoid arguing and getting angry. Your parents will be more likely to listen to you at a later time if you stay calm and respectful now.

Being Assertive for Real

Practice being assertive until it feels comfortable to you. Then try it out on some real-life situations. Start with something simple, like asking your little sister to leave your tapes alone, or telling your locker partner at school that you need more room on the top shelf. Follow the tips on pages 39–40 and you will increase your chances of success. Even if you don't always get what you want, you'll feel better about yourself for trying. Following are two more tips to boost your assertive advocacy skills.

Determine your strengths and weaknesses.

If you're going to advocate for yourself, you must know your strengths and weaknesses. After all, if you don't know your positive qualities, how can you communicate them to others? If you don't know your weaknesses, how can you improve?

Let's return to the curfew problem above. Before you talk to your parents, review your strengths and weaknesses. Do you keep your promises and do your chores at home without being nagged or reminded? Are you usually on time? Remind your parents of these strengths. On the other hand, do you often come home later than you promised? Have you gotten into trouble with the friends you hang out with? You probably need to improve on these weaknesses before you approach your parents. Otherwise, why should they give you extra privileges?

To be honest with your parents, you first need to be honest with yourself. You might make a list of your strengths and weaknesses. Discuss your list with someone you trust, and see if that person agrees or disagrees with your self-evaluation. You may have more strengths and fewer weaknesses than you think. For example, it takes courage to admit your weaknesses, even to yourself—and courage is a strength.

Be a good listener.

Gary says, "I once helped a student named Brenda to be an assertive advocate with her teacher. Brenda was getting behind in her homework because she always had more than she could handle. She felt that the teacher was assigning too much homework. Brenda's goal was to be allowed an extra day to complete some assignments. We listed her strengths and weaknesses, role-played some things she might say, and asked for a meeting with her teacher. At the meeting, Brenda did a great job of explaining what her problem was and outlining solutions. But whenever her teacher tried to say something, Brenda interrupted. She didn't listen to what her teacher had to say, and as a result, she didn't get what she wanted."

To be a successful advocate for yourself, you must also be a good listener. People are more likely to agree with you if they think you're hearing their point of view. They may have questions for you to answer or ideas for you to try; if you don't listen, you won't hear them. Brenda's teacher tried to ask her how much time she was spending on her homework, but Brenda kept interrupting. Then Brenda's teacher wanted to know how much time Brenda needed, but Brenda kept talking. Finally her teacher got frustrated and said "no" to Brenda's request for more time to do her homework.

REMEMBER

Assertive advocacy increases your chances of getting what you want and need. It helps you to feel good about yourself—stronger, more confident, in control of your life. It gives you a way to stick up for yourself without putting other people down.

GETTING A JOB: SHOULD YOU OR SHOULDN'T YOU?

Sometimes teenagers get fed up with school and studying all the time. They wish they could be more independent, have some money of their own, and stop depending on their parents for everything. They wish there was more to life than school. If you find yourself feeling this way, maybe you should get a part-time job.

Rhoda says, "My son, Carter, has LD. He is 27 years old now and has a good job working in a grocery store. He started working on a paper route when he was 12, and since then he has had many different jobs and learned a lot of good work habits. For example, he always arrives at work on time and he rarely misses a day. Carter is proud of himself for being so dependable, and he believes that his early jobs gave him the experience he needed to be a good employee. Not too long ago, Carter ran into one of his former employers, who offered to match his present salary and give him good benefits if Carter came back to work for him. Carter chose to stay with his present job, but having his skills recognized by his old boss was a boost to his self-esteem."

There are pros and cons—good things and bad things—about getting a job while you're still in school. We'll start with the good things.

Ten Reasons to Get a Job While You're Still in School

1. You'll learn things about the world of work that many people don't learn in school.

Can you perform several tasks simultaneously? Can you communicate effectively with customers? Organize your time? Be patient? Solve problems? Take instructions? Think on your feet? These are just a few of the skills you may learn and develop if you get a job.

2. Now may be an ideal time for you to try different jobs.

You may not have to support yourself, pay rent, or buy your own groceries—at least, not yet—so you can afford to try out different jobs. By the time you finish school, you should have some idea of the kind of work you like best.

If you're in junior high or middle school, or if you're just starting high school, many jobs will not legally be available to you because you're underage. You'll have to use your imagination and create your own jobs. For ideas and suggestions, see pages 65–71. If you're over 16, there are many different jobs you may want to consider; see pages 72–76 for tips on finding one that's right for you.

You should also consider volunteer work. You won't get paid, but you will learn job skills, and you will be appreciated. If you can't get a paying job—because you're underage, or for other reasons—volunteer work may be an excellent choice for you.

Rhoda says, "A young man named Jason started volunteering at day care centers when he was 13. At first he worked only during the summers, but when he started high school, he worked during the school year, too. After he graduated, one of the centers where he had volunteered offered him a full-time job."

There are many ways to find out about job opportunities. Ask your school counselor. Check with your local park director. Visit day care centers and nursing homes. Call community service organizations and find out if they need help. Ask your minister, rabbi, or priest for suggestions.

You may want to get a new job every summer or every school year. By the time you graduate from high school, you will have experienced many kinds of jobs, and you'll have a variety of skills to bring to a future full-time job.

3. A job will keep you busy and encourage you to organize your time and your life.

Sometimes teenagers get bored. They can't think of anything to do, especially during the summer when school is not in session. They spend their days watching TV, playing video games, or hanging out with their friends. Suddenly summer is over, it's time to return to school, and they haven't accomplished anything.

Having a job may prevent you from getting bored and it will also keep you busy. Busy people often learn to prioritize their activities and responsibilities so they can get everything done within a certain amount of time. They may learn to organize and manage their time. These are skills you'll use for the rest of your life.

4. A job will keep you away from the TV set.

Sometimes teenagers spend a lot of time in front of the TV. We know that TV can be relaxing, especially after a hard day at school, but we also know that you can get hooked on it if you're not careful. There is a balance between how much time you should spend watching TV and how much you should spend on other activities and pursuits. Having a job may help you to achieve that balance.

- Teenagers watch an average of 147 minutes of TV per day, or about 17 hours per week.

- By high school graduation, the average teenager has watched 20,000 hours of TV. That's more than he or she has spent in school and interacting with parents—combined.

- For many teenagers, TV has taken the place of other leisure activities. Instead of being with other people, doing things together and making friends, they're sitting home alone in front of the TV.

- Too much TV promotes a passive lifestyle. One study of 406 teenage boys found that those who watched little TV were more physically fit and active.

- The more time teenagers spend watching TV, the less time they spend reading and doing homework.

5. A successful job experience will help you to feel good about yourself.

To succeed at a job, you must discipline yourself to get enough sleep, look neat and presentable, say "no" to your friends when their activities conflict with your work schedule, and be responsible. These things add up to give you a feeling of pride and accomplishment at the end of the day.

If possible, find a job that doesn't require skills that are difficult for you because of your LD. For example, if you have a hard time reading, look for a job that doesn't require a lot of reading. If you have a language learning disability, you probably don't want to get a job answering telephones. If you have a perceptual motor disability, try to find a job where you don't have to do a lot of writing. Or ask if you will be writing on a computer.

One of the most satisfying feelings you'll ever experience is to go to bed tired because you have accomplished a lot. If you get up, go to school, go to work, come home and do your homework, then watch TV, listen to music, or talk on the phone for a while, you end the day knowing that you did everything you had to do and still had time left over for things you wanted to do. That's being in control of your life.

6. A job will make you more independent.

It's hard to depend on your parents for every dollar you need. When you want to see a movie, go out for a snack, get gas for the car, or ride the bus to the mall, it's always "Mom, can I have some money?" or "Dad, can I have a few dollars?" Maybe your parents give you an allowance for your spending money, but what if it isn't enough? What if they don't always remember your allowance?

Sometimes parents are happy to give you money, or they'll give it to you even if they aren't happy about it. But sometimes they may refuse your request. Maybe they're tired of being asked, or maybe they don't have any extra money to give you. If you have a part-time job, you'll receive a regular paycheck, usually every week or two. You'll know in advance how much money you'll earn and how much you'll have to spend. You'll be able to plan the things you need to buy, and you'll also be able to start saving money for larger purchases or future goals, such as renting an apartment or continuing your education beyond high school. Talk with your parents about how to manage the money you earn.*

7. A job will give you work experience.

Many young adults looking for full-time jobs find that employers want people with work experience. But you can't get work expe-

---

* For more tips on managing your money, see pages 58–59.

rience if you can't get a job. Having a part-time job as a teenager will give you valuable work experience.

You won't have your first part-time job for the rest of your life. You'll want to move on to different and better jobs. When you're ready to leave one job for another, ask for a letter of recommendation. You'll find two sample letters on page 54. If your employer has been happy with your work, he or she will gladly give you a letter of recommendation.

Bring along a photocopy of the letter when you interview for a new job. It will prove that you have work experience and that you're a good employee. Be sure to keep all letters of recommendation you receive while you're still in school, and make copies. They will help you to get a job after you graduate.

You should also prepare a resume—a summary of your work experience. You'll find a sample resume on page 55. On your resume, list any jobs you have had and describe your responsibilities. List the names and telephone numbers of your employers, present and past. Your resume should fit on one page; some employers won't read longer resumes. Keep your resume up-to-date, and bring it along to job interviews. It will show that you're serious about work.

If you need help preparing a resume, ask your school counselor or LD teacher.

LETTERS OF RECOMMENDATION

To Whom It May Concern:

John Smith was employed by Toolco Distribution Center #49 in Ann Arbor, Michigan, from May 25, 1987, until June 1, 1989. He started at $5.25 per hour and advanced through annual increases to $6.50 per hour. He was recognized by management because of his high productivity and accuracy on the shipping dock and because of his dependability for being at work.

Mr. Smith is welcome to return to Toolco, should he wish to do so, and I would recommend him to you as an excellent candidate for employment.

Jim Johnson
Personnel Manager

To Whom It May Concern:

Jenny Thomas began work as a receptionist for our full-service salon in October 1991. Her duties have included booking appointments; answering the phones; preparing schedules for the stylists, manicurists, and other employees; salon laundry and housekeeping; and public relations with the clientele. She has carried out these duties in a dependable and courteous manner.

We have been impressed with Jenny's maturity, sense of responsibility, and efficiency. We would recommend her highly as an experienced and capable employee. She will be a positive addition to any business environment.

Please feel free to contact me if you wish additional information.

Sincerely,

Mary Nelson, Salon Owner
Hair, Skin, & Nails Inc.

RESUME

Jenny Barbara Thomas

Address: 123 North Fourth Avenue #56, Chicago, IL
60605
Phone: (312) 555-6789
Birth Date: July 17, 1974
Social Security #: 555-55-5555

Education

Glenn H.S., Chicago, IL, 1988-1992.
Graduated June 1992.
Cook Jr. College, Chicago, IL. 1992-present.

Work Experience

October 1991—June 1992. Hair, Skin & Nails Inc.,
Chicago, IL. 555-0123/Mary Nelson, owner.
Made appointments, answered phones, helped with
schedules, did laundry, and greeted customers.

June 1991—August 1991. Kid Fun Summer School,
Chicago, IL. 555-4567/Terry O'Neill, manager.
Teachers' aide. Helped with 30-50 children who came
to summer school.

April 1990—July 1990. Biggest Burgers,
Chicago, IL. 555-8901/Rob Severs, supervisor.
Made hamburgers, fries, and shakes to fill customer
orders. Took orders and worked at the cash register.

Summers, 1986-1989. Tim Thomas, M.D.,
Chicago, IL. 555-2345.
Answered phones, checked in patients, did filing,
and helped the nurses prepare the examination rooms.
(Dr. Thomas is my father.)

8. A job may help you decide what to do after graduation.

Will you go to college, vocational school, or straight to full-time work? Maybe it's too soon to decide. But you will have to decide someday, and that day will come sooner than you think. Some teenagers find part-time jobs that they enjoy and keep all during school. After graduation, they become full-time employees of the same companies that gave them their first jobs. Or they may go on to college or vocational school for additional training related to that job.

Gary says, "Onika is a high-school senior who has been working in a veterinarian's office since she was 14. She loves her job, and she wants to be a veterinarian's assistant full-time after graduation. Onika plans to enroll in the community college and get an associate's degree as a veterinarian's assistant. Her employers have agreed to hire her when she finishes her degree."

You may not be as sure as Onika about what kind of work you want to do after graduation. However, part-time work may help you decide what kind of work you *don't* want to do, and this is important, too. You may realize that you need to go to college or vocational school for training in a different field. Or you may realize that you're not ready to make up your mind about a career. You may decide to stay in your present job full-time, save money, and wait until later to get more schooling. These are all good decisions.

9. A job will give you experience in getting along with others.

When you work, you have to get along with your employer or supervisor. Sometimes your employer may ask you to do more than you think you should have to do. Good workers are willing to do more than is expected of them, and they take pride in their work. They don't complain if their employer sometimes asks them to stay five or ten minutes late. They don't grumble if a coworker gets sick and they have to work harder. As long as you don't have to work overtime every day, or do someone else's job all the time, it's smart to help out. Many employers reward workers who make an extra effort. Of course, if these requests become unreasonable, you have the right to respectfully refuse.

You will occasionally make mistakes at work; everybody does. Good workers admit their mistakes and try to do better next time. They don't blame their mistakes on others. Employers appreciate workers who say, "I'm sorry. How can I fix my mistake? I'll try not to do it again."

Especially when you start a new job, it's important to follow instructions, work hard, be patient, and do your best. What if you don't agree with everything your employer says, and you don't understand why you're supposed to do something a certain way? Wait a while before you try to make changes. Do what you are told to do, as long as you are not asked to do anything wrong or illegal. Give yourself time to get used to your job and to learn your tasks and responsibilities. Something you don't agree with may start to make sense; something you don't understand may become clear to you. If you still have questions after two weeks or a month, talk to your employer or supervisor.*

When you work, you also have to get along with your coworkers. Sometimes people you work with may tease you or do other things to make you angry. Ignore them or tease back, but don't lose your temper. Just keep doing your job. Meanwhile, your coworkers will get tired of teasing you, and eventually they will stop. What if they don't stop? In the next chapter, you'll learn what to do about people who are cruel or abusive toward you.

10. You'll get paid for working.

Money is an important reason for working, but it's not the most important reason. Learning new skills, becoming more independent, and feeling good about yourself are also excellent reasons for having a part-time job.

What should you do with the money you earn? Spend it responsibly and save as much as you can. Some teenagers cash their paycheck on payday and spend all the money immediately. They buy things they don't need, eat out too much, or waste their money in other ways. Then they ask their parents for money to buy the things they need. This is not responsible spending. When you graduate from high school or college and start living on your own, you may get paid only once or twice a month, and you'll have to make your money last. Even if you work part-time, you should practice budgeting and saving the money you earn. ("Budgeting" means planning when and how you will spend your money, then sticking to your plan.) If you have trouble figuring out how to do this, ask your parents for advice.

---

* See Eight Tips for Talking to Teachers on pages 22–24. Modify them so they apply to your employer or supervisor.

One way to learn responsible spending is to cash your pay-check, divide the money, and put it into envelopes labeled "school supplies," "gas," "clothes," "movies," or whatever you plan to spend it on. (Or label the envelopes but keep your money in the bank.) If you put $10 in your movies envelope, spend that money only on movies; when it runs out, don't take money out of another envelope for movies. Wait for your next paycheck. If you have money left over when payday comes around, don't spend it on something else. Deposit it in the bank and save it. Later, when you are living on your own, you will remember how to budget and save money, and you will be less likely to spend foolishly or go into debt.

Five Reasons Not to Get a Job While You're Still in School

For some teenagers, a part-time job is just what they need. For others, there are good reasons to wait until after graduation before getting a job.

1. You may already be too busy.

Maybe you're on the football team, or perhaps you go to dance class three times a week after school. If you're already very busy, it will be hard to find time for a job, and you may have to give up some of your other activities first. Talk to your parents and decide together if going to work is worth giving up things you are already doing.

2. A job might interfere with your school work.

There are laws that limit the number of hours that teenagers can work. Most employers honor these laws, but some employers ignore them and make teenagers work longer hours than they should. Before you take any job, find out how many hours you will have to work each day, and think about the hours you must spend each day on school work. What will happen if you take the job? Will it cut into your homework time? Will you still have time for fun? Answer these questions as honestly as you can. You may decide that the job will fit in with the rest of your life, or you may decide to ask for fewer hours—or look for a different job.

Don't let a job take the place of your school work. You still need to do your best in school and graduate. Your job may seem more important than school, but it is not more important. Just ask someone who didn't graduate from high school.

"For most jobs, you need a diploma, not a GED." Juan, 16

"My mom dropped out of high school in 11th grade. She says she didn't want to learn anymore, but now I help her and she sometimes helps me. She told me to stay in school, but I think I'll drop out to be like her . . . . Just kidding!" Josh, 17

3. A job might prevent you from helping out at home.

Maybe your parents expect you to help with chores around the house. This seems reasonable. Why should they do all the work? As long as you live at home, you should help out. Maybe your parents really need your help, counting on you to care for your younger brothers and sisters or prepare the meals. If you get a job, your family will still need you to share in the chores at home. If you can, that's great; if you can't, you should wait to get a job.

4. Some jobs can make you feel bad about yourself.

Some teenagers end up in jobs that make them unhappy. Maybe they don't like the work they have to do, the people they work with, the hours, or the work environment. They start to feel bad about themselves because they are unhappy with their jobs.

Remember that a job should help you feel good about yourself. Before you take any job, learn as much about it as you can. Ask what you will be expected to do and talk to the person you will be working for. Ask yourself, "What will this job do for me? Will I learn new skills? Will it help me in the future?"

Rhoda says, "Daniel had a job cooking hamburgers. One day he accidentally dropped a whole tray of hamburgers on the floor before they were wrapped. The floor was dirty, but his supervisor made him pick up the hamburgers, wrap them, and sell them anyway. Some of Daniel's friends came in to buy hamburgers, and Daniel felt bad about selling them food that had been on the floor. He decided to look for another job—and to never eat in that restaurant again."

5. Some jobs require you to be dishonest.

If someone told you, "I have a great job for you! You'll make a lot of money fast," what would you do? We hope that you would say "no." In cases like these, follow this rule: If it sounds too good to be true, it is.

There are adults who hire teenagers to do work that is against the law. Obviously, selling drugs or stolen goods is illegal. Sometimes teenagers are tempted by these jobs because they think they can work for a little while, make a lot of money, and quit. But it's not that simple. An illegal job can get you in a great deal of trouble. It can be hard to quit—your "employer" may not let you quit—and it can be dangerous for you and other people. No amount of money is worth committing a crime, getting hurt, or hurting others. If you are ever asked to do work that is illegal, tell a parent, a teacher, or a counselor at school. Don't get mixed up in something you'll be sorry for later.

Making the Decision: To Work or Not to Work?

If you decide to get a job while you're still in school, you won't be alone. More than 5 *million* young people between the ages of 12 and 17 have part-time jobs.*

---

* On the down side, more than 71,000 teenagers were injured at work in 1990, according to the National Safe Workplace Institute.

You have read about ten reasons to get a job while you're still in school, and five reasons not to get a job until after you graduate. Let's find out what people who study teenagers are saying about this issue.

Researchers at Temple University in Pennsylvania wanted to find out what happened to teenagers who had jobs. They did a study of 1,800 high school students and discovered the following facts and trends:

- Teenagers who work a lot don't get involved in school activities. (Students who participate in school activities tend to do better in school.)

- Teenagers who work more than 15 hours a week have more problems than those who work fewer hours.

On the other hand, a 1991 study of high school students in California and Wisconsin showed that students who work a few hours a week actually do *better* in school than students who don't work at all. The key seems to be the number of hours worked. Teenagers who work from 1 to 10 hours a week are the most successful. Those who work more than 10 hours a week get lower grades, and their grades drop dramatically as their work hours increase. Students who work more than 21 hours a week have the worst grades of all. A study by the Educational Testing Service found that kids who work longer hours earn lower scores on math, science, history, literature, and reading achievement tests.

Getting a job is a big decision that we believe you and your parents should make together. Your parents may not want you to get a job because they think you would benefit more from school activities, or they may worry that you won't have time for friends and fun. Ask what else you can do to earn money for the things you need. Maybe your parents will give you a bigger allowance, or perhaps there are chores you can do at home for extra money.

Your parents may not want you to get a job because they think it will interfere with your school work. Do they have any reason to feel this way? How are your grades? Do you keep up with your homework, or do your parents have to nag you to do it? Do you finish school projects on time? Are you really mature enough to hold a part-time job without falling behind in school? Do you believe that a job will make you feel better about school and work harder to succeed? (School can be a drag, and a job may provide interest and excitement in your daily life that makes school easier to bear.) Spend time thinking about these questions and any others that occur to you, and write down your thoughts and responses. Then talk to your parents.

Tell your parents how you feel and ask if they will let you try working for a while. If your parents have worries or concerns, be willing to listen and negotiate. Tell your parents that you will stop working if your school work starts to suffer. Suggest that you will work for a trial period of six months. At the end of that time, you and your parents can talk about the advantages and disadvantages of your having a job. If you like your job and your grades have not gone down—or, even better, if your grades have gone up—your parents will probably be glad to let you keep working.

HOW TO FIND
AND KEEP A JOB

If you and your parents decide that it's okay for you to get a part-time job, what next? First, you have to find a job opening. Next, you have to apply for the job. Finally, if you get the job, you have to work to keep it. This chapter includes several descriptions of jobs you may want to consider.

Finding the Job That's Right for You: Tips for Younger Teenagers

Sometimes it's hard to find the job that's right for you. What kind of work should you look for? That will depend on

- how old you are,
- how much job experience you have,
- how many hours you want to work,

- what you like to do,
- how much time you need for activities other than school and work.

If you are a younger teenager with no job experience, finding the right job may be a special challenge. We recommend that you start with a simple job that won't take up too much of your time. Remember: When you leave a job, always ask for a letter of recommendation. It will help you to get your next job.*

Get a paper route.

This job may require you to get up early in the morning, usually around 4:30 or 5:00 a.m.** The newspaper delivers a stack of papers to your house or another location nearby, and you deliver the papers to the houses on your route. Usually, you are finished working by 6:30 or 7:00 a.m., and you never have to work afternoons or evenings. Once every month, if the newspaper doesn't bill customers directly, you may have to spend time going to the houses on your route to collect payment for the papers you deliver.

Gary says, "Jefferson is a 12-year-old friend of ours who has a paper route. He has figured out a way to collect payment without going from house to house. Jefferson addresses envelopes to each of the customers on his route. Inside the envelope, he places a copy of the bill and a stamped envelope addressed to himself. He leaves the bill with the newspaper on the first day of each month, and most of his customers mail their payments to him in the stamped envelope. He only has to go to a few houses on his route."

---

* See page 54 for sample letters of recommendation.

** Some newspapers publish afternoon editions. If you get a job delivering the afternoon papers, you can work after school. There are also jobs delivering community newspapers and advertising circulars for businesses and stores. These may have more flexible hours, and you won't have to collect from customers. Collecting can be a hassle.

House-sit.

Do your neighbors take vacations or business trips? Who watches their houses and takes care of their yards when they are gone? This may be something you can do. Create a flier advertising your services and charges, make several copies, and take them around your neighborhood. Be sure to include your name and telephone number. You might offer to collect the newspapers and mail, water the plants, mow the lawn, feed the fish, or do other chores that need to be done. Talk with your parents about how much to charge.

To get a job house-sitting, you will need to have a reputation for being mature and responsible. You will need to get good references from people other than your family members.

Baby-sit.

This is a tried-and-true way for younger teenagers to earn money, and it's not "for girls only"—boys can baby-sit, too. If you do a good job, your name will get around, and you may have more work than you can handle. Experienced and capable baby-sitters are always in demand.

Many communities offer special courses for teenagers who want to be baby-sitters. These courses teach you how to care for small children and what to do in case of an emergency. If you want to be a baby-sitter, you should plan to take one of these courses. When you complete the course, you will receive an official certificate. Teenagers who earn these certificates are in great demand as baby-sitters.

If you can't find a community education course on baby-sitting, check with the Camp Fire organization, 4-H, Red Cross, Girl Scouts and Boy Scouts, and your local YMCA or YWCA.

Before you consider baby-sitting, check out your own stress level around little kids. If they drive you crazy, baby-sitting may not be the right job for you. Kids take patience, kindness, understanding, and a *lot* of attention. Caring for them is hard work and a serious responsibility.

"I've just started baby-sitting for my neighbors' kids. I love it! Most of the kids are cool, and I have some extra money for a change." Shari, 13

BE A SUPER SITTER

How to Be a Super Sitter is a book-and-video training program for teenagers. It teaches you the basics of quality child care, child safety, and emergency procedures. You can learn a lot from this self-study course prepared by Dr. Lee Salk, a pediatrician and expert on children. To find out more about Super Sitters, write or call:

> Super Sitters Inc.
> PO Box 218
> Mequon, WI 53902
> (414) 242-2411

The Super Sitters training program is used by the YMCA, 4-H Clubs, Red Cross Agencies, hospitals, churches, medical clinics, and schools. You may want to call your local Y, 4-H, Red Cross, etc. to find out if it is offered in your area.

Do yard work.

Depending on where you live, yard work may be done only during the summer months. But if you work hard during the summer you might earn enough money for the whole school year. You will probably need your own tools—a lawn mower, clippers, and so on. Decide how much you will charge; yard work is usually done by the job, not by the hour. You may want to charge one price for just mowing the lawn and another (higher) price for additional work such as edging the yard, clipping around fences, weeding flower beds, and trimming hedges. Yard work offers another benefit: It's good exercise.

What can you do during the other seasons of the year? How about raking and bagging leaves, shoveling snow, and cleaning up the yard in the spring?

Take care of pets.

Sometimes pet owners go out of town or get sick, and they need temporary help caring for their pets. Elderly people may need help on a more permanent basis. Make fliers advertising the specific services you offer and list your charges. Will you feed pets? Will you walk dogs? Big, small, or all sizes? Will you spend time playing with pets who are left alone while their owners are away? Will you bathe or brush dogs and cats? In the future, you may want to work in a pet store or a veterinarian's office. Letters of recommendation from satisfied pet owners may help you to get the job you want.

Run errands.

If you live within walking distance of a grocery store or business district, take advantage of this money-making opportunity. Let your neighbors know that you're available to run errands. Do they need someone to make a quick trip to the grocery store? Buy stamps at the post office, or bring in a package for delivery? Pick up a book at a bookstore, or return books to the library? These are all things you could do to earn money.

People with disabilities sometimes need shopping assistance. They may need someone to go shopping with them, carry their purchases, and help them in other ways. Do you have a neighbor who is in a wheelchair? Someone who is visually impaired or partially sighted? An elderly neighbor who can't go shopping alone? Think of people who might need your help.

"I go down to the store to get groceries for my grandmother. She's in a wheelchair and can't go herself. She gives me $5 every time I go." G.W., 13

Invent your own job.

What are some services you could provide that other people would be willing to pay for? How about washing windows? Waxing cars? Painting fences? There are plenty of jobs that you can do. Use your imagination and be creative.

BE AN ENTREPRENEUR

An entrepreneur is someone who invents or starts a business. Check out these books for young entrepreneurs. Each one is full of suggestions and ideas for you to try. Remember: If you have trouble reading, get help.

■ *Teenage Entrepreneur's Guide* by Sarah L. Riehm. Surrey Books, 1990.

■ *Kid Biz: Year-Round Money Making Projects for Junior Entrepreneurs* by Bonnie and Noel Drew. Eakin Press, 1990. (An earlier edition of this book is titled *Fast Cash for Kids*.)

Finding the Job That's Right for You: Tips for Older Teenagers

You may already have some job experience. If so, that will make it easier to find the job that's right for you. Maybe you'll invent your own job; more likely, you'll look for a job that already exists. Following are suggestions on where and how to start looking.

Read the classified ads in the newspaper.

Look in the section called "Employment—Part Time" or find a section with a similar name. Read the ads every day for several days in a row. Sometimes a particular job will only be listed once, and sometimes it will be listed only on weekends or weekdays. When you find a job that looks interesting to you, circle it in red. When you have read the ads for two or three days, you will have circled many jobs. Go back and read them again. Make a list of the ones that look most interesting—your Top Five or Top Ten. If you have trouble reading the ads, get help.

Write down the specific things you must do to apply for each job. Does the ad say to call for an application or an appointment? Does it tell you to go to a certain place at a certain time for an application or interview? Follow the instructions exactly. If the ad says "no calls," don't call. If it says "come at 8:00 a.m. on Tuesday," don't show up at 10:00 a.m. on Friday. If it says "send a resume," then you know what to do.*

Tell friends who have jobs that you are looking for a job.

Many employers hire workers who are recommended by people already working for them. If you know someone who has a job

---

* See page 53 for suggestions on preparing a resume. A sample resume is found on page 55.

that you think may be right for you, ask if there are other openings there and see if your friend will put in a good word for you. Chances are, if your friend is a good worker, the employer will listen to the recommendation and invite you to come in for an interview.

"I got a great job at a record store because a friend of mine was quitting and told me to apply. He put in a good word for me . . . that was all it took." Timpko, 17

Go door-to-door.

The next time you have a day off from school or a weekend day free, go job hunting. Walk up and down a street and look at the different businesses. When you see one that looks interesting, go inside and find out if they are hiring. If the answer is "no," say "thank you" and go on to the next place. If the answer is "yes," you may be given an application to fill out, and you may even be interviewed on the spot.

Make it your job to look for a job. This is the way to get the best job for you. Many employers are impressed by teenagers who are brave enough to walk in and ask for a job. Also, appearance is important even when you're "just looking." Take time to be well groomed and neatly dressed. First impressions last.

Make a flier describing a service you can provide.

Can you baby-sit, house-sit, mow lawns, groom dogs, wash windows, clean houses, take photographs, shovel snow, wash cars, stuff envelopes, water plants, or rake leaves? Is there another service you can provide that people might be willing to pay for? Prepare a flier describing your services and charges. Include your name and telephone number. Include the name and number of an adult reference—someone who knows you and your work. (Get that person's permission first.) Take copies of your flier around your neighborhood. Post it on bulletin boards at local grocery stores and community centers. Mail it to businesses you think might be interested, or consider placing your own "Position Wanted" ad in your local newspaper.

Ask a teacher or another adult friend for ideas and recommendations.

Teachers and other adults are often aware of available jobs, and they may give you the names of businesses or individuals who are looking for part-time help. They may even agree to call an employer and recommend that you be hired. Think of the adults you know who may be willing to help you, and ask for their help. If your school has a career counselor, start there.

Impress somebody.

Rhoda says, "My son, Carter, got his current job by impressing somebody. One day we went grocery shopping together. When we finished at the checkout lane, all of the workers who bag the groceries were busy, so Carter grabbed a sack and started bagging our groceries himself. The checker noticed Carter and told him that the store was looking for good workers. He handed Carter an application and invited him to fill it out and bring it in the next day. He also said that Carter could use his name as a reference. Carter was hired almost immediately. His job at the grocery store pays well and the hours are great. Plus he has excellent medical and retirement benefits."

Gary says, "A friend of ours named Courtney has a job working as an aide in a summer-school program. She got the job because she started a conversation with the woman who ran the program. The woman was impressed with Courtney's self-confidence and friendliness. She asked Courtney if she would like to work for her, and Courtney said yes. Courtney loves her job, and she can't believe how easy it was to get."

You won't believe how easy it is to impress adults. Be friendly, be polite, and be yourself. Show that you aren't afraid of work and responsibility, and many adults will gladly give you a chance.

MORE ABOUT FINDING AND KEEPING A JOB

This chapter provides basic information about finding and keeping a job. There are many books and articles available with more detailed information, some of which were written especially for teenagers. Visit your library and ask the librarian to help you locate materials on this subject. If you have trouble reading, let the librarian know so he or she can find materials appropriate for your reading level. Or ask your school if they can get you a reader. Following are two titles we recommend.

A Real Job for You: An Employment Guide for Teens by Rose P. Lee. Betterway Publications, 1985. This very helpful guide takes you through every step of the job search process, from reading the want ads to interviewing effectively.

Teen Guide Job Search! 10 Easy Steps to Your Future by Donald L. Wilkes and Viola Hamilton-Wilkes. Jem/Job Educational Materials, 1992. A helpful guide with sensible advice, sample forms, basic tools, and self-quizzes for review. Write to Jem/Job Educational Materials, 1230 East Main Street, Alhambra, CA 91801.

Making the Decision: Important Questions to Ask

Let's say that you've found a job that seems right for you, and the employer has offered you the job. All you have to do is say "yes." Or maybe you have a choice between two or more job offers, and you can't decide which one to accept. Before you make a decision, take time to think it through. Following are five questions that can help you consider your choices and arrive at the right decision.

Are the hours reasonable for you?

Ask the employer to give you an idea of how many hours you'll be expected to work each day and each week. What days will you work? Will you work only on weekdays after school? How late in the evening will you work? What about weekends? Once you have this information, sit down with your parents and discuss whether the hours are reasonable for you. Make sure that your work hours won't interfere with time you need for school work and family or school activities. Work is important, but it's also important to balance work with other things you want and need to do.

Do you feel comfortable with the employer, the manager or supervisor, and the other workers?

Remember that you will have to get along with the other people at your workplace. Before you accept a job, spend some time talking with the employer. (In larger companies, you may never meet the employer. Talk to the person who would be your manager or supervisor.) Ask the manager or supervisor to introduce you to the other workers. Naturally, you can't really get to know people in a single meeting, but you might get a feeling for what it would be like to work with them. Do they seem friendly? Helpful? Patient and kind? If you don't feel comfortable with the people, you won't be happy with the job.

On the other hand, it's important to be realistic. You may not like everyone you meet, but you can still enjoy your work and do it well. You can still feel good about yourself.

Are your skills a good match with the job requirements?

Find out what you'll be expected to do, then think about what you're capable of doing. If the job looks too easy, you may get bored; if the job looks too hard, you may get frustrated. Either way, you won't be happy. Look for a job that will challenge you, but avoid a job that you know will be too difficult, demanding, or tiring for you. Choose a job that doesn't require skills that are hard for you because of your LD. Set yourself up for success.

Are your parents satisfied that the job is right for you?

Before you accept any job, talk about it with your parents or other adults you trust. Get their opinions on whether the job is right for you. Their opinions are worth hearing because they have had job experiences. Also, adults are more likely to support you if they feel the job is right for you. Their support will help you to succeed.

Does the job involve honest work?

Never accept a job that requires you to be dishonest or to risk hurting yourself or others. It just isn't worth it.

Gary says, "We know a young woman named Tina who made a very bad job decision. When she was 17, someone talked her into selling drugs to kids in middle school. Her 'employer' promised to pay her a lot of money for every sale she made. He also promised to pay her if she found other teenagers who were willing to work for him. Tina wanted many things, so she agreed to sell drugs as a way to earn money fast. For a while, she made a great deal of money—enough to buy new clothes, a stereo, and a car. After about a year, the police found out about Tina. They caught her selling drugs and arrested her. By then, Tina had turned 18, and she went on trial as an adult. She was found guilty of selling drugs to kids, and now she is in prison. Tina no longer has her clothes, her stereo, or her car. Kids got hooked on drugs because of her. She hurt herself and others. Tina's bad decision will affect the rest of her life."

Ten Tips for Keeping a Job

Some teenagers are successful at getting jobs, but they have a hard time keeping the jobs they get. We hope that when you get a job, you will be able to keep it for as long as you want it. We hope that when you leave your job, it will be because you are ready to leave, not because your employer has told you to leave. Following are ten suggestions for keeping a job.

1. Be enthusiastic.

When you get a job, appreciate it and show your appreciation. You may be competing with adults for the same job. If you are lucky enough to get it, be glad. No job is perfect, and there will be parts of your job that you won't like. Try to focus on the good parts and accept the rest as part of life.

2. Be dependable.

Your employer is counting on you. If you have to miss work for any reason, call your employer ahead of time and explain why you must be absent and when you can be expected to return. Missing work without calling in is an excellent way to get fired.

There are other ways to show that you are dependable. For example, don't be afraid to do more than is required. Volunteer to help out whenever you can. If your employer asks you to work on some holidays, do it if at all possible. You'll make a good impression and you'll probably earn holiday pay or overtime, which may be 1½ times more than you earn on regular work days.

Most employers reward dependable workers, as you'll discover for yourself when you ask for a raise, time off, or a letter of recommendation.

3. Be punctual.

Employees who come to work late and leave early are not good workers. Their employers don't respect them and their coworkers don't like them. If you arrive late, someone else has to do your work until you get there; if you leave early, someone else has to do the work you didn't finish. Arrive at work on time and stay until your shift is over. Show that you are part of the team.

"There was this guy at work who never could get there on time. He lasted about two weeks . . . that's it!" Shaun, 17

4. Dress well and be neat.

This is especially important if your job puts you in contact with the public. Are you the person behind the register or the counter? Do you take tickets or show customers to their seats? To the public, you represent the company you work for. If you are helpful and presentable, people will form positive feelings about your company. This brings in more business for your company and results in more appreciation for you.

Your employer may provide you with a uniform. Keep it neat and clean. If you don't have a uniform, wear clean clothes to work each day. Shower, brush your teeth, and use deodorant before you leave for work, and make sure that your hair is washed and combed. What if you get dirty on the job from frying hamburgers, cutting grass, or washing floors? You should still arrive at work neat and clean.

5. Be friendly.

Have you ever noticed that friendly people are people who have friends? A smile, a pleasant voice, and an outgoing personality can be very attractive. You probably know this from personal experience. You also know that everyone has days when things go wrong. You have a fight with your boyfriend or girlfriend. Your parents pick on you. Your dog chews your favorite shoes, or your bike gets stolen. Somebody calls you a name or spreads gossip about you. There's a problem in your family, you get in trouble at school for not turning in your homework—no wonder you feel sad or grumpy. But leave your sad, grumpy feelings at home. Don't bring them to work and take them out on your employer, coworkers, and customers. Other people shouldn't have to suffer just because you're having a bad day.

Of course, you shouldn't take out your bad feelings on your family, either. If you need help handling these feelings, talk to your LD teacher or the school counselor.

6. Do your best to get along with others.

It isn't always easy to work with other people. You may find that some have annoying habits that get on your nerves. They chew gum too loudly, laugh at everything, talk on the phone too much, or take too long to do their work.

It isn't always easy to work for other people. What if your employer asks you to do something you don't feel like doing? What if you don't like it when people tell you what to do? Maybe you're not mature enough to have a job.

If you want to keep your job, you need to get along with others, and you need to do what your employer tells you to do. If you get angry, you need to control your anger. It may be hard at first, but keep trying and soon you'll feel proud of your self-discipline.

Sometimes the people you work with may say or do something that makes you angry. Back off. Don't get into fights. If someone teases you, ignore it or tease back, and try not to be too bothered by the teasing. If you are bothered, try not to let it show. Some people will tease you even more if they know that it bothers you. What if you try everything—ignoring it, teasing back, trying not to let it bother you—and someone keeps teasing you anyway? Tell your employer about the problem and explain that nothing you do seems to work. This is not the same as tattling; you are telling your employer something he or she should know. Besides, it's better to talk about a problem before it gets even worse. If you don't talk about it, you might become so angry that you get into a fight. Fighting with other workers could get you fired.

Work hard, mind your own business, and show self-discipline. You will get along better with others and you will respect yourself.

7. Ask questions.

Sometimes teenagers get into trouble at work because they are confused. They may not know how to do a certain job, when to go to lunch, or when to take a break. They may not be sure about how to follow work rules. If there is something you don't understand, ask your manager or supervisor. Don't ask your coworkers. They may not know the answer, or they may give you the wrong answer. Most managers and supervisors will gladly help workers who ask questions.

Are you worried that your employer will think you are dumb? Asking questions isn't dumb. It shows that you care about doing things the right way, and you want to do your best. Asking questions means that you will make fewer mistakes on the job, and you will be a better, smarter employee.

8. Work, don't socialize.

It's important to be friendly when you are at work, and you may even make friends with some of the people you work with. But you're not getting paid to make friends, talk, and tell jokes. You're getting paid to work. If you want to have fun with the people you work with, plan to get together after work or on the weekend.

9. Don't be a whiner.

Some people complain about their jobs all the time. They complain about not getting paid enough, about the hours they have to work, about the customers and the boss, about anything and everything. They are a big pain, and they usually don't last very long before they are laid off or fired.

There are bound to be things you don't like about your job. If you think about them all the time, you will form a negative attitude, which will affect your ability to be a good employee. How can you do your best if you only see the worst? Focus on the positive parts of your job and try to ignore the negative parts.

10. Be a good quitter.

Someday you will quit your job. Make sure it's for a good reason.

These *are not* good reasons to quit your job:

- because you're tired of working,
- because someone at work has made you angry, or
- because you would rather go skiing.

These *are* good reasons to quit a job:

- because you have been offered a different job you want to take,
- because you are moving to another town or going away to college, or
- because your job is interfering with your school work.

As soon as you know you will be quitting, give your employer at least two weeks' notice. For example, if you want your last day to be Friday, November 20, tell your employer no later than Friday, November 6. This is the responsible way to quit a job. It gives your employer time to find someone to take your place.

Don't forget to ask for a letter of recommendation. If you have been a good employee and a good quitter, your employer will be glad to write a letter praising your skills and your performance on the job.

One final tip: If you decide to look for a different job, keep the job you have while you are looking. That way, you won't end up with no job.

WORDS OF WORK WISDOM

If you decide to get a part-time job . . .

- Make it your job to look for a job. It may take time to find the right job for you. Be patient and keep looking.

- When you get a job, appreciate it. There are many people who don't have jobs.

- Ask questions, ask for help, and don't be afraid of adults. (After all, you're almost an adult yourself.)

- Learn while you earn. Learn new skills and learn to get along with others.

- Working isn't for wimps. Are you responsible and mature enough to get and keep a job?

- Being a good employee proves that you are dependable and responsible. It proves that you can succeed in the world of work.

PLANNING FOR THE FUTURE: SETTING CAREER GOALS

Some teenagers graduate from high school with no clue about what they will do next. They think that they will just go to work, find someone to live with or marry, and start a family—not always in that order. We believe that it's important for all teenagers, especially teenagers with LD, to think first about their career goals. We believe that nobody should start a family without first getting established in a career. When you can live on your own, pay your bills, save money, and help to support a family, then you *may* be ready to start a family— not before. Working at a fast-food restaurant might be a good job while you are still in school, but it isn't likely to become a career unless you have the experience, education, and money to become the owner or manager.

WHAT STUDENTS ARE SAYING
ABOUT THEIR FUTURE

"I'm going to own my own special effects company and be an actor." Russ, 14

"I'm planning on going into the army." Eleanor, 16

"I'm going to be a chef." Raoul, 17

"I'm going to Southern Illinois University and play football, and then become a zoologist." Mathias, 18

"I want to be a landscaper." Cherilynn, 15

"I want to be a writer. Currently I'm taking a word processing class because my handwriting isn't good, and I want to be able to write on a computer." Elizabeth, 12

"I want to work in the field of electronics. Maybe I'll repair computers. Or maybe I'll design stereo equipment or video games." Ludlow, 13

"I want to be a pediatrician because I like little kids and I want to help them." Armand, 16

Five Ways to Learn about Careers While You're Still in School

How can you know which career is right for you? Start by thinking about some that might interest you. Which ones might use skills you already have? Skills you want to develop? What about your likes—and dislikes? Choose a few possibilities, then find out as much about them as you can. If you can't think of any interesting careers, find out about as many different ones as you can. Make learning about careers your first career goal.

Hint: Talk to your parents and other adults who know you well. Ask them to describe what they see as your strengths and weaknesses. Their perceptions may help to point you in the right career direction.

1. Try out several different jobs while you are still in school.

If possible, begin working as soon as you can. Start out with simple jobs, such as delivering newspapers, and gradually work your way up to more complicated jobs. Don't just go to work in a fast-food restaurant when you are 16 and stay there until you graduate. You'll learn a lot more about your own career goals if you try out several different jobs.

On the other hand, this may not always be practical. Sometimes jobs are hard to get. Also, there's a lot to be said for finding and keeping a steady job you enjoy.

2. Ask your school counselor or teacher to give you a career assessment.

A career assessment usually involves special tests called work interest inventories. They are fun and interesting to take—your counselor or teacher can give them to you—and you won't be graded on them. A work interest inventory gives you insights into your personality, your likes and dislikes, and your work interests, and describes jobs that are likely to be a good match.

One of the best work interest inventories is called *The Self-Directed Search (SDS)*. Developed by John Holland, it is appropriate for teenagers who are 14 and older. If you have trouble reading, ask to take *The Self-Directed Search, Form Easy*

(SDS-E). It provides the same information as the SDS, but it is easier to read. Also available is a computerized version of the SDS that will give you a 10- to 15-page printout of information about jobs that may be right for you. To find out more about the SDS, call 1-800-331-8378 toll-free, or write to:

> Psychological Assessment Resources, Inc.
> P.O. Box 998
> Odessa, FL 33556

To find out about other work interest inventories, talk to your LD teacher or school counselor.

3. Contact community agencies that can help you to make career-related decisions.

Some examples are

- the state employment agency,
- the state vocational rehabilitation agency,
- private employment agencies,
- community colleges,
- junior colleges,
- trade and vocational schools,
- four-year colleges and universities.

Spend time visiting these agencies and schools. Talk to their counselors and employment specialists, and find out all you can about the work-assistance programs that are available to you. If you are getting special education services because of your LD, you may be eligible for special help from some of these agencies. Ask your special education teacher or school counselor to tell you about these.

4. Read catalogs from community and junior colleges, trade and vocational schools, and four-year colleges and universities.

Your school may have several catalogs available. Ask your school counselor or teacher if you can borrow them, or write to the schools and request your own copies. If you don't have the addresses you need, go to the library and ask the librarian to help you find the addresses. When you have the catalogs you want, spend some time looking through them. If you have trouble reading, get help. Find out what programs and courses are offered. If you see something that interests you, ask your school counselor how you can get more information about it. Go the library and ask the librarian to help you learn more about your area of interest.

5. Talk to people who work in different jobs.

Are you interested in working with animals? Then talk to people who work with animals in their jobs. Visit a pet store, meet with a dog groomer, and request permission to spend a day observing a veterinarian at work. Make a list of questions you would like to ask these people about their jobs. For example:

- "What kind of training and education does your job require?"

- "Are there any risks associated with your job? What are they?"

- "About how much money can someone earn at this job? What is the starting pay? About how much does this job pay after five years? After ten years?"

- "How many hours a day do you work? Do you work evenings and weekends?"

- "What does someone have to do to succeed at this job?"

Ask your teacher, counselor, or parents to help you prepare your list of questions. Tape record the answers people give you (with their permission) and review them at a later time, or take careful notes during your conversation.

You may want to schedule informational interviews with employers. For each one, make an appointment and arrive on time, with a list of questions you have prepared. If you like, and if it's okay with the employer, bring a friend or adult along for help and support. If you need assistance setting up interviews and thinking of questions, ask your school guidance counselor or special education teacher.

REMEMBER:

The more you can find out about yourself, your personality, your likes and dislikes, and your work interests . . .

The more you can find out about the job possibilities available to you . . .

The sooner you start . . .

The better your chances of finding the right career for you.

For more advice on career choices, see if your library has one or both of these books. If you have trouble reading, ask for help.

- *The College Board Guide to Jobs and Career Planning* by Joyce Slayton Mitchell. The College Board, 1990. Describes more than 100 occupations from A (accountant) to W (writer) and tells you how to prepare for them. Lots of specific information, very well organized.

- *Exploring Careers*, revised edition. JIST Works, Inc., 1990. Write to: JIST, 720 North Park Avenue, Indianapolis, IN 46202-3431. Describes over 300 jobs. Includes career exploration activities and worksheets. Based on information from the U.S. Department of Labor.

After-Graduation Opportunities

What will you do when you graduate from high school? Will you go to work full-time right away? Will you get special training in a job or skill? Will you go to college? Depending on your career goals, your skills, your work experience, and your personal circumstances, you may have many possibilities to choose from. Plan ahead!

Perhaps you received special training in high school on car engines or computers. If so, you may be ready to start working full-time. Perhaps you want to be a court reporter or a flower arranger. If so, you will need special training at a community college or junior college. If you want to be a school teacher, you will have to go to a four-year college or university. Following are several employment, training, and educational options for you to consider.

State and private employment agencies.

If you want to start working full-time as soon as you finish high school, and if you are not already working in a job that you want to stay in, pay a visit to an employment agency. Both state and private employment agencies have lists of employers who are looking for workers.

State agencies usually list federal, state, or city government jobs, or jobs that require manual labor. They provide their services for free. Private agencies are more likely to represent private firms and businesses, and they charge a fee for their services. Sometimes the employer pays the fee; sometimes the employee pays the fee. If you find a job through a private employment agency, you may have to spend most of your first paycheck or more to pay the fee.

The state vocational rehabilitation agency.

Are you or have you ever been in the special education program at your school? If the answer is "yes," then you are eligible for special help from the state vocational rehabilitation agency when you graduate. The agency can't find you a job, but it can provide you with services you need to get a job, including financial assistance and counseling. It may also provide you with special technology you need because of your disability. For example, if you want to be a truck driver, the agency may pay your tuition at a truck drivers' school. If you need to improve your math skills to keep the job you have or get a better job, the agency may pay a math tutor to help you. Or it may pay your tuition for a math course at a community college or junior college. If you need a computer with software that talks, the agency may provide you with one to use on the job.

Trade and vocational schools.

These state-supported or private schools provide training in job-related skills. Some examples of trade and vocational schools include:

- a truck drivers' school,
- a business college,
- a two-year school that offers training in auto mechanics, computer-assisted design (CAD), or drafting.

Students at trade and vocational schools learn specific skills needed for specific jobs. If you go to a business college, you won't learn how to be a truck driver. If you go to a school that teaches you how to be a radio announcer, you may not learn much about banking. So it's important to choose your school carefully. Talk to people who have gone there, and ask the school how many of its graduates get jobs related to their training. If they can't tell you, try another school.

No trade or vocational school can guarantee you a job when you graduate. But some schools have higher success rates than others, meaning that more of their graduates get jobs. These schools are usually happy to share these facts and figures. Be careful of schools that make promises without any proof.

FIND OUT MORE

Two books to look for in your local library:

- *Getting Skilled, Getting Ahead: Your Guide for Choosing a Career and a Private Career School* by James R. Myers, Ph.D., and Elizabeth Warner Scott, M.A. Peterson's Guides, 1989. Good advice about trade schools, vocational schools, and business schools.

- *How to Choose a Career and a Career School for the Student with a Disability.* National Association of Trade and Technical Schools. Write to NATTS, 2251 Wisconsin Avenue NW, Washington, DC 20007. Advice for students with all kinds of disabilities and differences.

Community and junior colleges.

These colleges usually offer a two-year associate's degree in some specialized area. For example, if you want to be a licensed child-care aide, court reporter, or veterinarian's assistant, then you will probably need an associate's degree in your chosen field. Community and junior colleges also offer one-year training programs. For example, if you want to be a flower arranger or assistant to an interior decorator, consider signing up for one of these programs.

Many community and junior colleges offer a two-year, pre-college course of study. During this time, you take general education courses that help to prepare you for a four-year college or university. Some students go to a community college or junior college for their first two years of college course work, then switch to a four-year college or university for their final two years. This makes college seem a lot easier.

Four-year colleges and universities.

You may decide that you want to get a college degree. Many students with LD go to college and graduate. If you meet the requirements for admission, college may be a good choice for you. The admission requirements may be very strict, and you may need to take special college entrance exams. Your high school grade-point average (GPA) will have to be a C-plus or better, and your entrance exam scores will have to be at or above a certain cutoff point.

Four-year colleges and universities can be stressful. (This is true for all students, not only students with LD.) There is competition to get in and competition to stay in. The homework, assignments, and tests can be hard. But if you want to go to college, then go for it. Ask your school counselor or teacher for help and advice about colleges and universities. Several have special programs for students with LD. Ask your counselor or teacher what exams you need to take and arrange to take them. Find out when you need to apply for admission and how to complete an application form.

If you are worried about going to college but you would like to earn a college degree, try this: Enroll first in a community college or junior college for a couple of years. Their classes are usually smaller, their instructors are more understanding and available to help, and their counseling centers are equipped to provide special assistance for students with LD.

Before you enroll in a community college or junior college, check with the four-year college you think you will want to attend. Find out which community/junior college credits can be transferred to the four-year college. For example, if you take a junior college math course for 3 credits, will the four-year college accept those credits? If not, you may have to take the course again at the four-year college. This takes time and costs money. Also, find out from the four-year college which courses you should take before you arrive. Then you will be ready to be a third-year college student.

Every college has basic requirements. These are courses they expect every student to take, in addition to special courses required for his or her major. Most students complete these required courses during the first two years. If you spend the first two years at a community college or junior college, you will want to be sure to take as many of the required courses as you can.

MORE COLLEGE KNOWLEDGE

- Many four-year colleges and universities have special programs for students with LD. Some schools are known to have better support services than others. For help in locating these colleges, ask your LD teacher or write to:

LDA
4156 Library Road
Pittsburgh, PA 15234

or

National Center for Learning Disabilities Inc. (NCLD)
99 Park Avenue
New York, NY 10016

Request information about colleges for people with LD.

■ Find out more about colleges by writing to:

American Council on Education
One Dupont Circle NW, Suite 800
Washington, DC 20036-1193

Ask for their paper called "Learning Disabled Adults in Postsecondary Education." They will send you one copy for free.

■ Look for these helpful books in your library:

Guide to Colleges with Programs or Services for Students with Learning Disabilities by M. Lipkin, 1990. Write to Schoolsearch Press, 127 Marsh Street, Belmont, MA 02178.

The K & W Guide: Colleges and the Learning Disabled Student: A Reference/Resource Book for Students, Parents, and Professionals by Marybeth Kravets and Imy F. Wax, 1991. Write to Kravetz, Wax & Associates, Box 187, Deerfield, IL 60015.

National Directory of Four-Year Colleges, Two-Year Colleges, and Post High School Training Programs for Young People with Learning Disabilities by P.M. Fielding and J.R. Moss, updated often. Write to Partners in Publishing, Box 50347, Tulsa, OK 74150.

Peterson's Guides to Colleges with Programs for Learning Disabled Students by Charles T. Mangrum II, Ed.D., and Stephen S. Strichert, Ph.D. Peterson's Guides, updated often.

GETTING READY
TO LIVE ON YOUR OWN

Many teenagers with LD tell us that they can't wait to get out of school and live on their own. Some even drop out of school, get a full-time job, and move out of their parents' house because they are so eager for their independence. We believe it is a bad idea to drop out of school for any reason. You may find a job, but it probably won't pay much, and it won't offer much of a future. Then what will you have? Your independence, a dead-end job, and not even enough money to live on. You may decide to return to school later, but it's much harder to go back and finish than to stay in and finish.

Good jobs offer regular pay raises, opportunities for advancement to better positions, and health and retirement benefits. These jobs are harder to get than dead-end jobs, and most require at least a high school diploma. So our advice to teenagers is always to complete high school. This may be very hard for you to do; it may seem as if school will last forever and you'll never have your independence. But staying in school now will pay off in the future, because you'll have a better chance of getting a good job and earning enough money to support yourself. That's real independence, and it's worth waiting for.

Many teenagers believe that if they can just move out of their parents' home, they will be more independent. We believe that moving out before you are ready might make you less independent than you are now. Have you thought about how much it will cost to rent an apartment and pay for heat, electricity, and telephone service? To buy your own groceries, dishes, and cooking utensils? To pay the insurance and maintenance for a car? To pay doctor and hospital bills if you get sick? Will you have the money for all of these things and more?

Sometimes being independent means being tied down to bills, bills, and more bills. You can't achieve real independence until you have a job where you earn enough to meet your monthly expenses, buy essentials (clothing, groceries, car insurance, gas), and still have money left over to spend on fun. What about movies, music, eating out, and vacations? You're not really independent if all you can afford to do is stay home.

Some teenagers who get an allowance from their parents or work at a part-time job get to spend their money on whatever they want. They take it for granted that their parents will pay the rent or make the house payment, buy the groceries, pay the car insurance, and take care of the other monthly bills and purchases. Someday soon, ask your parents how much it costs to run the house for a month or a year. You will be surprised by what you hear.

Eleven Steps toward Real Independence

What is the best way to achieve real independence? Be patient. Try to get along with your parents, take your school work seriously, and graduate from high school. Then you and your parents will have more confidence in your ability to live on your own. Some teenagers go to work full-time as soon as they graduate from high school, while others go on to a trade school, college, or university. No matter what you decide to do in the future, there are some things you can do now to prepare to live on your own.

1. Work to earn an allowance, plan to save part of it, and spend the rest wisely.

Make a list of chores you can do every week to help out around the house. Ask your parents if they will give you a weekly allowance for doing the chores. If they agree, decide together how much you should earn. Be ready to compromise; your parents may not be willing to pay you as much as you want. Maybe you can offer to do more chores in return for more money.

Plan to save part of your allowance every week, and form a habit of saving *at least* that much each week—more whenever you can. Meanwhile, set a personal goal of buying something you really want, such as a portable stereo, athletic shoes, or a new jacket. After you have saved money for several weeks, take part of your savings and buy the item. But don't touch the rest of your savings. Leave it alone until you graduate. Keep it in a bank account that earns interest—a percentage the bank pays you for keeping your money there. Ask your parents or another adult to help you find a bank that pays a good rate of interest on savings accounts. The more money you save now, the more you will have later.

Make a list of things you will purchase with the part of your allowance you plan to spend. These should not just be fun things, like cassettes, video games, or clothes. Your list should also include some necessities that your parents have paid for in the past, such as toothpaste, deodorant, and haircuts.

Divide your weekly allowance into three parts: money to be saved, money to be spent on necessities, and money to be spent on fun and entertainment. This is how you will budget your money in the future, when you are living on your own, and it's smart to start practicing now.

2. Get a job.

Chapters 4 and 5 discuss how to go about getting a job. Read them carefully, then find a job that is right for you at this particular time in your life. Divide your earnings into three parts: savings, necessities, and fun.

3. Open a checking account.

Ask your parents to help you find a bank that will let you open a checking account, and deposit part of your allowance or earnings into your account. Each month, write one or two checks to pay for things you need or want. Be sure to write down the check numbers and amounts. Your checkbook will include a check register booklet for recording the checks you write.

You will need to learn how to balance your checkbook. Ask a parent or another adult for help. Or make an appointment to see a customer service representative at the bank where you have your checking account. He or she will walk you through every step of balancing your checkbook. Some banks will do this for free, others for a small service charge. If you like, bring a friend along who already understands the process and can help you to ask the right kinds of questions.

4. Watch your parents pay the bills.

Ask your parents if you can sit with them sometime and watch them pay the monthly bills. Have a calculator handy and add up the checks they write. You'll be surprised at the amount of money your parents must spend cach month just to keep up with the bills.

5. Go grocery shopping.

Ask your parents to let you do the grocery shopping sometimes. Have them make a list of the things you should buy, estimate the total cost, and give you enough money to pay for everything on the list. For the first time or two, ask them to make a *short* list so you don't get discouraged.

See if your parents will make a deal with you: If you can buy everything on the list for less than their estimate, you get to keep the difference. This will give you an incentive to be a careful shopper. To find the best bargains, visit two or three different stores, write down the price of each item on the list, and compare prices. Shop at the store or stores where you can save the most money. If you need help learning how to comparison shop, have an adult go with you once or twice. Hint: Generic brands are often less expensive than brand-name items.

You may be able to do some of your shopping before you leave home. Look for coupons and sale ads in the newspaper and scan advertising circulars. See if any of the coupons or sale ads match items on your list. Write down the prices and store names next to the items, clip the coupons, and shop at the stores that offer the best prices.

6. Look for coupons to save money on things you buy.

There are coupons for many things besides groceries. Examples: pizza, oil changes, haircuts, dry cleaning. The Sunday and Wednesday newspapers usually have the most coupons. Look for ones that will help you save money on things you need to buy now or in the near future. Cut them out, save them, and use them when you have the chance. Separate the coupons with expiration dates (the ones you must use by a certain time) from those with no expiration dates (the ones you can use anytime). For each item you purchase with a coupon, compare the original cost with the cost listed on the coupon. Figure out how much money you saved by using the coupon.

7. Take your parents out to dinner.

Use part of your savings to take your parents or another adult out to dinner. You don't have to go to an expensive restaurant, but you should go someplace where you can place your order with a waiter. As each person orders, check the prices on the menu and write them down. Add them up to find the total cost of the meal. When the waiter brings the check after the meal, ask the percentage of the tax. Multiply the total cost of the meal by the percentage of the tax. Does your number match the amount of tax listed on the check? Does your total for the meal—including the tax—match the total on the check?

Figure out the tip. The usual amount is a percentage of the bill, not including the tax—for example, 15 percent. Multiply the total cost of the meal by .15 and add that amount to the total on the check. Take the check to the cashier and pay the bill.

Example:

Steak	$7.95
Spaghetti	4.95
Soup	2.95
Subtotal	15.95
Tax =	
6% of 15.95	.95
Tip =	
15% of 15.95	2.39
Subtotal	15.95
+ Tax	.95
+ Tip	2.39
TOTAL	**$19.29**

If it's all right with your parents, take responsibility for figuring out the check whenever you go out together to eat.

8. Learn to cook.

Ask your family if you can help with the cooking sometimes. At first you may just want to watch your mother or father prepare the meal. When you feel that you know what to do, ask if you can prepare a meal by yourself. Start with a simple dinner—maybe some pasta and bottled sauce. Later, try preparing a meal from scratch. As you become more comfortable and confident in the kitchen, you can fix more elaborate meals. You may surprise yourself and discover that you enjoy cooking and you're good at it.

9. Find out how to rent an apartment.

Look for the classified ads in the newspaper and find the section titled "Apartment Rentals." Read the ads (or have someone read them to you) until you find one for an apartment that appeals to you—one you might want to live in if you were on your own. Call the number listed in the ad, ask to speak to the manager, and ask specific questions about the apartment. For example:

- "How many bedrooms does it have?"

- "How much is the rent?"

- "Who pays the utilities?" (The utilities include electricity, water, and heat. The tenant always pays for his or her own telephone.)

- "Do you require a deposit?" (A deposit is money you pay up front. It guarantees the apartment until you move in, pays for any damages that may occur while you are living there, and covers the cost of cleaning the apartment when you move out, if necessary. A usual deposit is one or two months' rent.)

- "Do I need to sign a lease? How long is the lease period?" (A lease is a legal agreement stating that you will live in the apartment for a minimum amount of time, usually six months or a year.)

- "Do you allow pets?" (Some apartments do and some don't. Those that do might specify a certain kind of pet. Examples: a cat, a bird, a dog that weighs less than 15 pounds.)

These are all questions you will need to ask when you are ready to get your own apartment, and it's wise to practice asking them in advance. Write down all the costs that the apartment manager tells you about. Call several apartment managers and ask them the same questions. You will find that different apartments have different rules.

10. Call the utility companies.

Some apartment rents include the costs of heat, electricity, and water, but most don't, and you'll have to pay these costs when you live on your own. Learn as much about them as you can. Call the gas company, the electric company, and the water company and find out the average costs per month for a one-bedroom, one-person apartment. If they don't give out averages, ask friends who rent apartments what they usually pay.

You'll probably want a telephone, so call the telephone company and ask about the connection and monthly service charges and any deposits they require. Call the cable company and find out how much it costs to start service, pay the deposit, and pay the monthly fee.

When you have finished making your calls, add up all the numbers. This is approximately how much you will have to spend each month to turn on the lights, watch TV, use the telephone, and so on. Is it more or less than you expected?

11. Learn to manage your time.

Buy a pocket calendar with lots of writing space. Each day, write down the things you have to do and the places you have to go. For example, you might want to write down the date a paper is due, when you are going to a movie with a friend, and the time you are supposed to begin your babysitting job on Friday night. Write down birthdays, other special occasions, and personal goals—things you want to do or achieve by a certain date. Look at your calendar every day to make sure you remember to do the things you want and need to do. Also, look a few days ahead so you can plan for upcoming events. When you accomplish a task or meet a goal, cross it off on your calendar.

A calendar will help you organize your time and gain control over your life. You'll be less likely to forget deadlines and appointments, you'll arrive at places on time, you won't feel as rushed or pressured, and you'll enjoy a sense of accomplishment whenever you cross off a task or a goal. On days when you feel discouraged about something you *didn't* get done, write down on your calendar any extras you did.

How to Win Your Parents' Confidence

You may feel ready for all kinds of responsibilities, and you may want to try some of the steps toward independence, but your parents may not agree. They may be reluctant or unwilling to let you do new things because they think you're not ready yet or they're afraid you might get hurt. Sometimes parents of teenagers with LD are overprotective; they think you're less capable than you really are just because you have LD. If your parents are like this, it's not because they're mean, they don't trust you, or they think you're still a baby. They love you, they want the best for you, and they want to keep you safe for as long as they can. Meanwhile, you feel smothered and wish you had more freedom.

We believe that teenagers with LD should have the same chances as other teenagers to explore their independence. If we could talk to your parents, we would encourage them to let you try some things on your own.* That's because we know many teenagers with LD, and we have confidence in them. We know they can make good decisions if they are given the chance. But we also understand your parents' concerns because we feel the same way about our own kids.

Rhoda says, "I still try to interfere with Carter's business, and he's 27 years old. He just tells me not to worry so much. I still worry some—that's the way parents are—but I also have confidence in Carter, and I know he can take care of himself."

---

* Since we probably won't have the chance to talk to your parents, how about showing them this part of the book? Then talk over the issues together.

Do you think your parents are overprotective? Following are some tried-and-true ways to win their confidence and increase your freedom.

Earn their trust.

First and most important, be honest with your parents. Many teenagers lie to their parents about where they are going and who they are going with, what they are doing or what they have done. When parents learn that their children have lied to them, their trust is destroyed. It only takes an instant to destroy a parent's trust; it may take weeks, months, or longer to restore it. If you lie to your parents and they find out, they won't forget it anytime soon. Whenever you ask for more responsibility or independence, they will remember the lie.

If you want your parents to trust you, don't lie. Sometimes telling the truth may get in the way of something you want to do. Sometimes it may even get you into trouble. Still, you should always ask yourself if it's worth telling a lie and getting caught. The answer will probably be no, so tell the truth and take the consequences.

Most parents are willing to give their children more freedom if they feel that they can be trusted. Telling the truth builds trust, and the more your parents trust you, the more freedom you will probably have.

Negotiate, don't argue.

Sometimes teenagers will ask their parents if they can stay out late or take the car and their parents will say "no." When they hear the word "no," they start to argue with their parents. Arguing is one of the worst ways to win your parents' confidence. It's true that sometimes parents say "no" without thinking, and this can be annoying. If you believe that your parents are being unreasonable or unfair and you have a good reason for making your request, try to negotiate with your parents. Work toward an agreement that is acceptable to everyone, and be ready to compromise.

For example: It's Friday night, and you want to borrow your parents' car to take yourself and three friends to a basketball game and out for pizza afterwards. You have a good reason: you're the only one of your friends who has a driver's license. Tell your parents the facts and ask if you can borrow their car. Explain where you want to go and who will be going with you. Your parents may say "no" because they are afraid that you're not responsible enough to take the car out alone. Negotiate, don't argue. Explain that you would like to have the chance to prove that you are responsible. Tell your parents what times you will leave and return home. Offer to fill the car with gas before you go.

Your parents may decide to let you take the car to the game if you come straight home afterward, without stopping for pizza. This is a compromise you can probably live with. Agree to their terms and honor your part of the bargain; don't stop for pizza even if your friends beg you, tease you, or try to convince you. If your parents see that you can keep your word, they will have more confidence in you, and they may be willing to negotiate with you again in the future.

Hint: If you know you're going to need the car, try to ask your parents at least two to three days in advance. Then they won't feel pressured and they'll have time to think it over.

Ask them to give you a chance.

Every once in a while, ask your parents to let you prove that you are responsible. Ask them to give you a chance.

For example: A group of your friends has invited you to go to the mall with them. One of them is a person your parents don't approve of because they believe he or she is a bad influence. Tell your parents that you understand their concern but you'd like to have a chance to prove that you can think for yourself. Say that even if someone in your group wants to do something wrong, you won't go along.

If your parents agree to let you go to the mall, be sure to do the right thing no matter what. Remember that your parents gave you a chance and don't blow it. When they understand that you can act responsibly, they will realize that you make your own decisions and you are not easily influenced by your friends. Your parents will have more confidence in you and give you more freedom.

"I used to get in trouble all the time. It wasn't my friends' fault; it was my fault for listening to them. They told me to do things and I did them. I wanted to be what they wanted me to be. But now I'm myself—I do what I think is right, and I don't let them influence me." Poco, 16

Ask them to let you make some decisions.

Do your parents tell you what clothes to wear and how to get your hair cut, when to go to bed and who your friends should be? Before long you'll be on your own, and you'll have to make these decisions (and many more) by yourself. You need some practice now.

We believe that teenagers should make their own choices about hair styles, clothes, bedtimes, and other day-to-day issues as long as they don't hurt themselves or other people. For example: You want to go to bed at 11:00, but your parents go to bed at 10:00. If you make so much noise between 10:00 and 11:00 that you keep your parents awake, you are hurting them. If you can't stay awake in school, you are hurting yourself. In either case, an

11:00 bedtime is not a good idea for you. However, if you are quiet after 10:00 and you are not tired in school, a later bedtime seems reasonable.

If your parents see that you can make good decisions about relatively small issues like this one, they will have more confidence in you, and they may start letting you make decisions about more important things.

Show them that you are responsible.

Think of things you can to do help out without being asked or told. For example, you might mow the lawn, clean the house, prepare dinner, or do the laundry. Don't ask for anything in return. If you surprise your parents by taking more responsibility, they may surprise you by giving you more freedom.

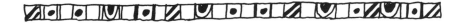

"Whenever I borrow my mom's car, I get it home on time if not earlier. Whenever I tell my parents I'm going to be home at a certain time, I keep my promise. Before I used to hang out with my friends, skip school, come home late, and do things I wasn't supposed to do. Things are different and better now." Casper, 18

"My parents and I get along. I took a lot of responsibility and earned their respect." Elsa, 14

LEARNING TO GET AROUND ON YOUR OWN

Do you always ask your parents to take you places? Do you expect them to drive you everywhere you want to go? Learning to get around on your own is another important step toward independence.*

Riding the Bus

Sometimes people think that the only way to get around is by car. But if you're a teenager, you usually can't drive until you turn 16, and what if your parents won't let you borrow their car? We believe that even younger teenagers can learn to ride the bus. Then they don't have to bother their parents for rides all the time.

---

* This chapter is about learning to use public transportation and drive a car. But there are other ways to get around on your own. You can ride a bike, skate, or walk, depending on how far you need to go. You can arrange to ride with friends who drive. If you do this often, be sure to pay for part of the gas.

Charlie is 13, and he rides the bus everywhere. He learned to ride the bus during the summer after sixth grade. His parents are divorced and his mother has a job, so Charlie was spending days at home alone. Before long, he grew bored, and he wanted to go places and do things, but there was nobody around to drive him. Then one day Charlie saw a TV commercial about the city bus company. He learned that there were summer passes available for kids who wanted to ride the bus. Charlie called the number given on the commercial and asked for more information about the program. When the information came in the mail, Charlie showed it to his mother, and they sat down together and studied it. They learned how to get the summer passes and how to read the map showing the different bus routes. Charlie told his mother that if she would let him ride the bus to places like the swimming pool, the movie theater, and the bowling alley, he would promise to be responsible. He would always tell her where he was going and when, and he would come home on time.

Charlie's mother agreed to let him try riding the bus if he followed two rules: First, he always had to ride with a friend, and second, he could never ride the bus after dark. Charlie agreed to his mother's rules. By the end of the summer, he was an expert bus rider, and his mother was proud of him for being so independent.

If you are responsible enough to ride the bus, and if your parents agree, then you should learn this important skill. Following are some guidelines and precautions to keep in mind.

Make sure that you understand the schedule.

Do you know how to read a bus schedule? If not, you will need to learn. Start by deciding where you will ride the bus—two or three places you will want to go most often. Then call the bus company. Tell them where you live and where you want to go. Ask them to send you the right schedules. Or stop in at a public library or shopping mall; bus schedules are often available at those places.

Find out the number of the bus that will take you to each destination. Do you know what time it leaves and arrives? Will you have to transfer to another bus somewhere along the way? Are the bus routes marked "N" (North), "S" (South), "E" (East), or "W" (West) and do you know which one to take? Ask a friend or adult to ride the bus with you once or twice until you understand the different routes and procedures. Then your parents will feel more confident about letting you ride the bus on your own.

Ride with a friend.

We believe that younger teenagers should always ride the bus with a friend and never ride alone. If something happens to one of you, the other can call for help. We don't think it is ever a good idea for younger teenagers to ride around town by themselves.

Don't talk to strangers.

Lots of different people ride the bus. Most of them are nice people who use the bus for transportation. However, if you don't know a person, you can't tell for certain whether he or she is nice. For that reason, we think it's best if you don't talk to strangers. Instead, wait patiently at the bus stop for the bus to come. Get on the bus, pay your fare, find a seat, and stay quiet until you arrive at your destination.

You may want to bring along something to do—a magazine to read, a crossword puzzle book, your cassette player and a tape.

(However, *don't* get so involved in what you're doing that you forget to pay attention and miss your stop. Sometimes bus drivers call out stops, but sometimes they don't.) If someone starts talking to you, say a few polite words and go back to what you were doing. This will usually discourage people from trying to make conversation. If you feel that someone is bothering you, move forward in the bus until you are sitting as close as possible to the driver. Tell the driver if someone keeps bothering you and won't leave you alone.

Have your pass or the right change ready.

Make sure you know how much the fare will be and have the right change ready when you enter the bus. In most cities, bus drivers won't make change. If you plan to ride the bus often, buy a pass that will let you ride as often as you like. Then you won't have to worry about having the right change.

Tip: A pass may be too expensive if you don't ride the bus every day. In some cities, you can buy books of coupons to use for riding the bus. Find out the choices available to you, then decide which one is least expensive.

Don't hang around the bus station.

Depending on where you ride the bus, you may need to transfer to another bus at the station or transportation center. Sometimes young people hang out at bus stations, and you might be tempted to hang out with them. However, drug dealers and other criminals may also hang out there. We think it's best to make your transfer without stopping to talk to other people, including your friends. It's okay to say "hi" and chat briefly, but don't stay around the station unless you're waiting to transfer.

Traveling Long Distances

Someday you might take a long trip by yourself on a bus, train, or airplane; maybe you already have. We believe that responsible teenagers should be able to take long-distance trips on their own. Your first trip may be exciting, even scary, but after you travel by yourself a few times you'll feel more confident and comfortable. Following are some suggestions for keeping travel safe and fun.

BEFORE YOU FLY

If you're planning a trip by airplane, you may want to send for "Kids and Teens in Flight." This free checklist includes a take-along travel card for recording flight information, emergency telephone numbers, and other important information.
Write to:

U.S. Department of Transportation
Room 10405, I-25
Washington, DC 20590

Know where you are going.

Are you visiting a friend or a relative? Write the person's name, address, and telephone number in your calendar or on a piece of paper for your wallet or purse, and keep it with you at all times. Are you going to camp or meeting a group? Write down the director's name, address, and telephone number and keep it with you.

Get help making connections.

Depending on where and how far you travel, you may need to change buses, trains, or planes somewhere along the way. Find out ahead of time how to make connections. Ask questions if you're not sure. For the first couple of times you travel alone, your parents may ask an employee of the company to help you make your connec-

tions. Write the name of the person on your ticket, in your calendar, or on a piece of paper to keep in your wallet or purse.

Ask questions.

If you are ever traveling by yourself and you are afraid that no one is going to tell you what you need to do, ask questions. Maybe you don't understand how you are supposed to change to another plane, or maybe you don't know where to go to pick up your luggage when you arrive at the airport or station. While you are still on the bus, train, or plane, ask the driver, porter, or attendant what you are supposed to do. If you don't understand the answer, repeat the question. Keep asking until you get an answer you understand. If you still aren't sure what to do or where to go, ask the person to show you. Never guess. Always ask.

Bring enough money.

Whenever you travel alone, be sure to bring enough money to cover your needs during the trip. Will you pay for meals, watch a movie on the plane, or take a taxi from the station or airport to your final destination? Keep change for telephone calls separate in case you need to make a call from a pay phone. Never leave for a trip without enough money to handle emergencies. However, be sure not to carry *too* much cash. And keep it in two different places. If part of your money is lost or stolen, you'll still have some left. Suggestions: Keep some in your wallet or purse, and some in a "tummy pack" fastened around your waist. Or wear a small coin purse on a leather thong around your neck and tuck it inside your clothes. Or carry travelers's checks instead of cash.

Some teenagers are authorized to use their parents' credit cards for meals, purchases, and telephone calls. See if your parents will allow you to carry credit cards when you travel as a safety net.

Don't talk to strangers.

If you don't feel comfortable going to the bus station, train station, or airport by yourself, ask an adult to go with you—at least for the first time or two. Ask the adult to wait with you until it is time for you to leave.

If you go by yourself, don't talk to strangers while you are waiting to leave. Once you are on the bus, train, or plane, it's probably okay to talk to the passengers sitting next to you, as long as you don't bother someone who is trying to read, work, or sleep. However, if anyone ever says or does anything that makes you feel funny or uncomfortable, call the porter or attendant immediately and ask to be moved to a different seat.

Learning to Drive a Car

Many teenagers get along just fine riding the bus or getting their parents to take them places. Even so, most teenagers want to learn to drive and get their license as soon as they reach legal age. We believe that most teenagers with LD can learn to drive, and we encourage their parents to let them. However, we also believe that only responsible teenagers should be allowed to get a license. It isn't enough for you to think you are responsible. Your parents should feel the same way about you. An automobile can be a very dangerous machine. Tens of thousands of people are killed each year in automobile accidents, and most deaths are caused by irresponsible drivers, including

- drivers who have been using drugs or alcohol,
- drivers who aren't paying attention,
- drivers who are sleepy,
- drivers who go too fast,
- drivers who go too slow (far below the speed limit),
- drivers who don't obey traffic signs and signals,
- drivers who use their cars to show off in front of their friends,
- drivers who try to get back at other drivers who make them angry.

A car can give you a lot of freedom, but you need to understand the responsibilities that go along with that freedom. If you want to learn to drive, and if your parents agree that you are ready, follow these suggestions for becoming a responsible driver.

Take a driver's education course.

In most states, people who are old enough to drive can get a license without taking driver's education course. However, we believe that all people should take driver's ed, especially teenagers. If your school offers driver's ed, be sure to take it before you graduate. If driver's ed is not available at your school, ask your teacher or counselor to help you explore alternatives. Private driving schools offer the course for a fee.

Driver's ed is usually divided into two parts, classroom instruction and driving instruction. In the classroom, you learn the safety rules and rules of the road, which prepares you to take the written test required for your learner's permit. During driving instruction, you get actual practice driving a car, with the instructor beside you. By the end of the course, most students are ready to take the written and driving tests at the State Department of Motor Vehicles. You must pass both tests to get your license.

If you have a hard time learning the material in the driver's ed course offered at your school, your parents (or you, if you are 18 or older) have the right to ask for modifications in the way the material is presented. You may want to include these modifications in your IEP. For the written test, your instructor and the State Department of Motor Vehicles should make any modifications necessary to make sure you can understand written questions. Ask your instructor how to request the state modifications. If you take a course from a private business, check to see if they will make modifications before you pay for the course. You may need help from your teacher or counselor to find a business that will make the modifications you need.

Concentrate on your driving.

We have an friend who took his eyes off the road to change the tape in his car cassette player. It was only a second or two, but it was long enough for his car to swerve to the right, and he hit and killed a bicycle rider. *Never* take your eyes off the road while you are driving—not to change a tape, dial a car phone, eat a taco, talk to a friend in the back seat, or for any other reason.

Never drink and drive.

You should not drink alcohol at all until you reach legal age in your state. Even then, you should never drive after you have been drinking any amount of alcohol. You could easily have an accident and seriously injure or kill yourself or another person. Or the police might stop you, charge you with a DUI (Driving Under the Influence), arrest you, and put you in jail. Alcohol and cars don't mix, so don't make a mistake you might regret for the rest of your life.

Obey the speed limit.

Many teenagers like to drive too fast because it makes them feel powerful and brave and they think it impresses their friends. Most accidents teenagers have are the result of speeding. Showing off in a car is never a good idea.

Always obey the speed limit, even if you are late for a meeting, an appointment, or a date. Driving too fast may get you killed. And how much time will you really save? Imagine that you are driving down a road where the speed limit is 30 miles per hour. You have 5 miles to go, so it will take 10 minutes to get there. Because you are worried about being late, you decide to drive twice as fast—60 miles per hour. If you don't cause an accident or get stopped by the police, it will take 5 minutes to reach your destination, saving you just 5 minutes. Is it worth the risk?

Respect your parents' property.

After you get your driver's license, and before you get your own car, your parents may let you borrow their car once in a while. If they do, they are trusting you to take care of it. Driving off the pavement is hard on a car, and so is driving too fast and squealing around corners. Respect your parents' property and their trust in you. Take good care of their car when you are driving it.

Buy your own gas.

If you drive your parents' car, buy your own gas with your allowance or work earnings. Gas is expensive, and your parents shouldn't have to pay for what you use while you are driving their car.

Maintain the car so it lasts longer.

If you drive your parents' car, offer to pay for an oil change once in a while, or learn to change it yourself. If you own your own car, be sure to change the oil and get a tune-up on a regular basis. If you take care of these small things, your car will last longer and expensive repairs may not be necessary.

DRIVING DO'S

DO . . .

. . . take driver's education

. . . learn and obey the rules of the road

. . . obey the speed limit

. . . concentrate on your driving

. . . keep your eyes on the road at all times

. . . obey traffic signals

. . . be a safe driver

. . . be a sober driver

. . . be an alert and awake driver

. . . respect your parents' property

. . . buy your own gas

. . . help to maintain the car

. . . remember that driving is an adult responsibility.

MAKING AND KEEPING FRIENDS

Gary says, "I first met Morgan a few years ago, when he was 14. His family had just moved to California, and Morgan had to start a new school in the middle of the school year. He was nervous and eager to make friends. On his first day, some kids in one of his classes started talking about leaving school during lunch and drinking beer. They asked Morgan if he drank, and Morgan said 'Yeah, all the time,' even though he had never drunk alcohol before. Morgan just wanted to be accepted. He went with the other kids at lunch and drank two beers. When the other kids told him to go to a store and steal some more beer, Morgan did it and was caught. He was placed in a juvenile detention center.

"I met Tasha at around the same time. She was 16, and like Morgan she had moved to a new school in the middle of the school year and wanted to make friends. She asked her school counselor and me to introduce her to some other students. She told us that she was into sports, especially softball and basketball, and she described the kind of music she liked. We asked some students to show Tasha around. By the end of the day, she had some new friends to hang out with, and by the end of the week, it seemed like Tasha had been at the school all her life."

Facts about Making Friends

Making friends is harder for some people than it is for others. Morgan was shy and quiet, while Tasha was outgoing and friendly, so it was easier for Tasha to make friends than it was for Morgan. But even if you are more like Morgan than Tasha, you can still make friends. Following are three important facts to keep in mind.

Everyone wants friends.

You may feel that nothing is more important than having friends. You may think that it is better to have some kids to hang out with, even kids who get in trouble, than to have nobody. Morgan learned the hard way that these are the wrong friends to have. Making the right friends takes time, and you may have to be alone for a while until you find the right friends.

LD doesn't have to get in your way.

Teenagers like to fit in. They don't like anything that makes them seem different from everyone else. You may not want to go to LD classes because it makes you seem different. Perhaps you think that if you didn't go to LD classes, it would be easier to make friends. You can't do anything about the fact that you have LD, but you can do something about your attitude—the way you feel and act about your LD. Tasha had LD, and she didn't let it get in her way. Her attitude was, "Hey, I have LD. So what? It's part of who I am. If you don't want to be friends because of it, then I don't need you for a friend."

Some "friends" are not really your friends.

Think about the people you call your friends. Think about what happens and how you feel when you are with them. Then decide if they are really your friends. Morgan thought he had made some new friends, but all they wanted was to use Morgan to get more beer.

If someone is always encouraging you to do things that get you in trouble, or things you don't want to do, he or she is not your friend. People who put you down are not your friends. If someone only wants to be with you when you have money, food, or the use of your parents' car, that person is not your friend. Do any of these sound like the people you hang out with? You may need to make different friends. It will take time, and you may feel lonely for a while, but be patient until you meet someone who is really your friend.

Ten Tips for Making and Keeping Friends

1. Ask for help.

Tasha asked Gary and her school counselor to introduce her to some students at her new school. Is there someone you know who might help you to meet new people? What about a teacher you respect? A school counselor? Your parents or other relatives? Your minister, priest, or rabbi? We realize that it's hard to ask for help, and it's hard to find someone you think will understand. If you can't think of anyone to ask, look around your school. Which teachers or other adults do students like to talk to? Which seem the most friendly and willing to listen? Perhaps you can ask these adults to introduce you to some other students.

2. Keep your eyes and ears open.

You may not know at first which students you would like to be friends with. Watch and listen during lunch, and before and after school. Is there someone else who seems to need a friend? Is there a group of students from one of your classes who seem friendly? Is someone involved in an activity that seems interesting to you? These are all good possibilities for friends.

3. Become an expert.

Is there a subject, activity, or hobby that other students your age are interested in? Would you like to know more about it? Then become an expert. It may be music, in-line skating, cars, motorcycles, baseball cards, movies, or almost anything. Learn as much about it as you can, and when you hear other students talking about it, join in. If you're an expert, you'll have something to contribute, and you'll feel more confident about taking part in the conversation. However, don't act as if you know *everything* about the subject. Be willing to listen and learn from others.

4. Join a group or club.

Find a group or club that matches one of your interests. Many groups welcome new members. Look around your school, church or temple, or community for possibilities to explore. Examples might include language clubs, service groups, and athletic teams at your local park. Talk to your LD teacher or school counselor about groups and clubs at your school. Ask your rabbi, minister, or priest about groups in your community, or visit a park and talk to an employee about opportunities there.

A GUIDE TO NATIONAL CLUBS AND ORGANIZATIONS

Directory of American Youth Organizations by Judith B. Erickson, Ph.D. Free Spirit Publishing, updated often. This book lists and describes 500 clubs, groups, organizations, and more for young people. You'll find hobby groups, political organizations, sports organizations, and much more.

5. Take a risk.

If you stand around waiting for people to come to you, it will take a long time to find friends. Why don't you make the first move? We know how scary this can be. What if you start talking to someone who makes fun of you or tells you to get lost? That happens sometimes, and it hurts. On the other hand, that person may want to be friends with you, and you'll be glad you took the risk. Taking risks takes courage, and there are no guarantees that you will get what you want. But how will you know unless you try?

6. Choose your friends carefully.

Juanita wanted friends very badly. She noticed that Cheri was popular and got a lot of attention from the other students. Juanita tried to get Cheri to pay attention to her, but Cheri ignored her. Finally Cheri said something cruel to Juanita. Naturally, Juanita felt embarrassed and hurt. Has this ever happened to you? Maybe you would like to be friends with the most popular students in your school, and maybe you have tried and felt rejected. Look for other students who would make good friends. The shy teenager in your math class may be waiting for someone like you to make the first move.

7. Listen.

When you find someone to talk to, remember to listen as well as talk. Everyone likes to be listened to, so if you are a good listener, you will find that people will want to talk to you. If most of your sentences start with "I," you need to practice listening. Of course, your friends should also listen to you. You should not be the only good listener in your group.

8. Give and take.

There should be times when you do favors for your friends, and times when they do favors for you. If a friend buys you a soda, buy one for him or her the next time you're out together. Don't take advantage of your friends, and don't let them take advantage of you. Find a balance between giving and taking. This is a good way to keep friends.

9. Leave some space.

When you make a new friend, it's easy to go too far. You may call your new friend several times a day and try to spend all of your time together, especially if you don't have other friends to hang around with. This is a good way to lose friends. If you are too demanding, you may push your new friend away. If you are jealous of the time your friend spends with other people, you may not be friends for long. Leave some space in your friendship for other people and for yourself. This will also give you the opportunity to make more friends.

10. Value yourself.

The best way to make and keep friends is to value and respect yourself. People like to be with people who like themselves and have positive self-esteem. There are many ways to show that you value yourself: by keeping yourself neat and clean, being true to yourself and your beliefs, staying healthy, choosing your friends carefully, being trustworthy and responsible, and making a contribution to your community because you know you have much to offer. If you need help learning to value yourself—if your self-esteem is low or nonexistent—tell an adult you trust. Many teenagers put themselves down, so you're not alone. But you do need to tell someone who can help you to see what a worthwhile and valuable person you are.

Sometimes teenagers think that if life is the pits today, it will stay that way forever. That just isn't true. Things change, and they can change for the better. If you're not happy in school, keep telling yourself that you *will* graduate someday. When you do, you may discover that the world is a much more interesting and friendly place than school ever was. You may find friends in many places: at work, in your neighborhood, at the club or gym where you go to work out. School is only a part of your life. There's more to come.

WISE WORDS ABOUT FRIENDSHIP

"Some people are so anxious to make new friends that they never have old ones." Aesop

"Treat your friends as you do your pictures, and place them in their best light." Jennie Jerome Churchill

"It is better to be alone than in bad company."
George Washington

"If I don't have friends, then I ain't got nothin.'"
Billie Holiday

"A friend is a present you give yourself."
Robert Louis Stevenson

"Good friends are good for your health." Irwin Sarason

"No person is your friend who demands your silence, or denies your right to grow." Alice Walker

DATING AND BEYOND

You may get special help in school because of your LD. In most other ways, though, you're just like most other people your age. You want to have friends, you want to be liked, and you want to do what other people your age are doing. Maybe you have had a girlfriend or boyfriend, or maybe you have one now. Perhaps you have gone on dates or thought about dating. You have probably thought about the future and wondered about marriage and having children. You may be curious about sex or think about it a lot.

This chapter is about these important topics. Since subjects like dating, sexuality, and marriage are very personal, we encourage you to talk about them with your parents or other adults you trust. Your family probably has opinions on these subjects and we hope you will listen to their opinions.

LD and Decisions about Dating

While the fact that you have LD doesn't affect your desire to date, your sexual feelings, and so forth, it may affect the decisions you make in these areas. For example:

- Some people with LD are impulsive. They may do or say things without thinking them through. If you are impulsive, you could make some poor choices about dating, sexuality, or marriage. These choices could have serious consequences for your life.

- Some people with LD have a social perceptual disability, and they make mistakes about the way other people feel about them. Imagine that you want to date someone at your school but that person ignores you or treats you unkindly. If you have a social perceptual disability, you may have trouble figuring out that this person doesn't want to date you, and ignoring you or being mean is a way of letting you know.

- Some people with LD feel that their LD makes them different from everyone else and less desirable as a boyfriend or girlfriend. They may be afraid that nobody will ever like them. If you feel this way about your LD, you could decide to date someone who isn't right for you out of fear that nobody else will ever ask you. Be patient, work on building your self-esteem, and wait for the right person. Meanwhile, it's better to be alone or spend time with friends than to go out with the wrong person.

Following are three tips that will help you to make good decisions about dating.

Make careful choices.

Ester was a 15-year-old who didn't have many friends. She was impulsive and she had a social perceptual disability. She felt lonely and wanted a boyfriend. One day Ester walked up to a group of young men at her school and asked one of them if he wanted to be her boyfriend. The boys laughed at Ester and made fun of her, and Ester felt embarrassed and even more lonely.

Ester did not make a careful choice. Because she was impulsive, she asked the first person who looked good to her if he wanted to be her boyfriend. Because of her social perceptual disability, she did not think about the fact that the young man was with a group of his friends. Even if he liked Ester, it was the wrong time to ask him to be her boyfriend.

How can you make a careful choice about a boyfriend or girlfriend? Start by asking yourself these questions:

- Is this person friendly to me?
- Does he or she like to talk to me?
- Do we like to talk about and do the same things?
- Is this someone I feel comfortable with?
- Is this someone I feel safe with?
- Is this someone I know, or would like to get to know better?

If your goal is to date only popular and good-looking students, even if they are unfriendly to you or ignore you, then you will probably be disappointed.

If at first you don't succeed . . .

It feels miserable to ask someone out for a date and be turned down, but it happens to everyone sooner or later, and it doesn't matter if you have LD or not. Because it hurts to be rejected, you may decide that it's easier to be by yourself and never ask anyone out. This is a great way to stay lonely.

If you make careful choices, the people you ask out will be more likely to say yes. But even if they say "no," don't give up on dating. Continue making careful choices and asking people out, and you will find someone who wants to go out with you. Meanwhile, talk to an understanding friend, a counselor, or another adult you trust about how it feels to be turned down. Ask for information that might help you in the future. Is there something you say or do that turns people off? Are there are things about yourself that you could work on and improve? Afterward, make another careful choice and try again.

Avoid risky situations.

Going on your first date with someone you really like is an exciting experience. You'll probably spend a lot of time thinking about it before it happens—what you will wear, what you will do, what you will talk about. Even if you have made a careful choice, there are some risky situations you should avoid. They could get you in trouble and turn your first date into a bad experience.

- Avoid places where you will be all alone with your date.

Stay in public places as much as possible—movie theaters, bowling alleys, skating rinks, concert halls, restaurants, and so on. This gives you a chance to get to know your date better before being out alone together.

Even if you believe that your date is someone you can trust, stay on the safe side. Also, you are less likely to be attacked or robbed if you are in a public place, so it is safer for both of you.

- Avoid doing things that make you feel uncomfortable.

What if your date takes you to a party where people are using alcohol or drugs? What if your date wants to have sex with you, and you don't want to have sex with him or her? These are tough situations to be in because you want to have fun and be accepted. You may be afraid that your date won't like you if you don't go along. What should you do? *You have the right to say "no" to anything that feels uncomfortable to you.* Follow this guideline: If it doesn't feel right, it isn't. Chapter 3 tells you how to be an assertive advocate. Read the chapter carefully, role-play tough situations, and decide what you would do in real-life situations. You can't control the fact that some people won't want to date you if you refuse to drink, use drugs, or have sex. You may feel bad about saying "no," but you will feel much worse if you do things that aren't right for you.

Sexual Feelings and Behaviors

Having LD means that you learn some things differently from other people. It doesn't mean that you come from a different planet. Remember that you're a lot like most other people your age, and you have the same feelings—including sexual feelings. Maybe you think about sex a lot, and maybe you have fantasies and daydreams about sex. All of this is normal for someone your age. Sexual feelings can be very powerful. While having LD doesn't affect your sexual feelings, it may affect what you do about them.*

---

* Alcohol and drugs also affect your sexual feelings. Read about alcohol and drugs on pages 160–161.

Do you remember Ester, the impulsive young woman with a social perceptual disability who wanted a boyfriend? One night Ester went to a roller-skating rink where a lot of teenagers hang out. Outside the roller-skating rink was a large park with many trees and private places. Three boys from Ester's school started teasing her and daring her to go into the park with them. Ester felt uncomfortable, but she didn't know why. Because of her social perceptual disability, she couldn't tell if the boys were making fun of her or if they really liked her. She wanted attention from boys, and even teasing seemed better than being ignored, so Ester acted impulsively. She went with the boys and had sex with each of them. Word got around, and soon a lot of boys were using Ester for sex. Ester got pregnant and she also contracted a sexually transmitted disease called herpes.

You probably think that you would never act like Ester, and you are probably right. But remember that sexual feelings are very powerful, as is the need to be liked and accepted. These feelings and needs can get you in trouble before you know it. Ester never meant to get pregnant, and she never meant to get herpes. These things happened because Ester made bad decisions about sex. Following are two suggestions that will help you to make good decisions about sex.

Talk to an adult you trust.

If you have any questions about your sexual feelings, please talk to an adult you trust, preferably before you get into situations where you feel pressured to have sex. It's hard to say "no" to sexual pressure, especially when your own sexual feelings are strong.

Educate yourself.

Go to a library and check out books and articles about the dangers and responsibilities of sex. On pages 141–142, you'll find a list of materials we know and recommend. Use this list as a starting point. New materials are always being made available.

If you need help finding books and articles you want to read, ask the librarian. If you have trouble reading, ask if the library has talking books on the subject, or get a reader. If you are too embarrassed to ask the librarian, ask a friend or trusted adult to find the materials for you.

One final word about sexuality: If you decide to say "no" to sexual activity until later in your life, you know that you will be safe from unwanted pregnancy and sexually transmitted diseases, at least until that time. If you decide to have sex, find out how to avoid pregnancy and diseases before you start. If you are already having sex, find out now.

FIND OUT MORE ABOUT SEX AND SEXUALITY

BOOKS

- Bell, R. *Changing Bodies, Changing Lives.* Random House, 1980.

- Blake, Jeanne. *Risky Times: How to Be AIDS-Smart and Stay Healthy.* Workman, 1990.

- Comfort, A. and Comfort, J. *The Facts of Love.* Mitchell Beazley Publishers, 1979.

- Hofstein, S. *The Human Story.* Lothrop, Lee & Shepard, 1967.

- Madaras, Lynda. *Lynda Madaras Talks to Teens about AIDS.* Newmarket Press, 1988.

- Madaras, Lynda. *The What's Happening to My Body Book for Boys.* Newmarket Press, 1988.

- Madaras, Lynda. *The What's Happening to My Body Book for Girls.* Newmarket Press, 1988.

- Marsh, Carole S. *Sex Stuff for Kids 7-17.* Gallopade Publications, 1987.

- Masland, Robert. *What Teenagers Want to Know about Sex: Questions and Answers.* Little, Brown, 1988.

- McCoy, K., and Wibbelsman, C. *The New Teenage Body Book.* Putnam, 1992.

- McCoy, Kathy. *Growing and Changing.* Putnam, 1986.

- Nourse, A. *Menstruation: Just Plain Talk.* Franklin Watts, 1980.

- Pomeroy, Wardell Baxter. *Boys and Sex.* Delacorte, 1991.

- Pomeroy, Wardell Baxter. *Girls and Sex.* Delacorte, 1991.

PAMPHLETS

- Berg, E. "Teens and AIDS: Why Risk It?" Santa Cruz, CA: Network Publications, 1987. Write to P.O. Box 1830, Santa Cruz, CA 95061-1830. Or call (408) 438-4080.

- Chiapelle, J. "Talking with Your Teenager about AIDS." Network Publications, 1988.

- Hiatt, J. "Deciding about Sex: The Choice to Abstain." Network Publications, 1986.

- Stringer, G. "Date Rape: Terri and J.R. Talk to Teens." Network Publications, 1986.

Marriage and Children

You probably aren't thinking about getting married and having children right away, but we want to say a few things about those subjects anyway. If you're not dating already, you probably will be in the near future. You'll be making choices about the kinds of people you spend time with. If you make good choices now, you are more likely to make good choices in the future, when you may decide to get married and have children. If you are impulsive, or if you feel lonely and unloved, you may make poor choices now and in the future. The difference is, if you make a poor decision about a date, you don't have to go out with that person again. If you make a poor decision about marriage and children, it will have consequences that last a lifetime.

You may have fantasies about marriage and children, based on what you have seen on TV or in movies or magazines. Perhaps you dream about a life with a husband or wife and two or three children where everyone is always happy and you are never lonely. If you are unhappy at home, you may think that marriage and children are a way to escape. The idea of sleeping with someone you love and having children to hug and kiss may seem very appealing.

Marriage and children can be satisfying and rewarding for mature people, but there is a big difference between real life and what you see on TV, in movies, and in magazines. Talk to adults who have been married for some time and ask them what it takes to make a marriage work. Talk to adults who have been divorced to find out what problems can develop in a marriage. Take a marriage and family course if one is available at your school. If your school doesn't offer such a course, sign up for one at a community center, community college, church or synagogue. Learn as much as you can about marriage before you get married.

If you think you want children someday, get some experience dealing with babies and very young children. Spend some time with the children of your adult friends, neighbors, and relatives. Ask your friends, neighbors, and relatives what it is like to raise children. If there is a day care center in your neighborhood, ask if you can visit and talk to the staff about what it takes to care for kids. Or volunteer there to get firsthand experience caring for children. If you have younger brothers and sisters, you may already know what it's like to be around children. Talk to your parents about the problems, joys, and frustrations of raising you and your brothers and sisters.

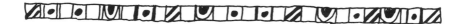

WHAT STUDENTS ARE SAYING ABOUT
RAISING CHILDREN

"When I'm a senior, I'm going to take a child development class." Pauline, 15

"When I have kids, I'm going to go places with them, not just stay at home and watch TV." Stan, 14

"I won't let my kids do whatever they want. I plan to teach them to be caring and responsible." Ashley, 12

"If my kids need help learning to swim or doing their homework, I'll help them. If they have problems, I'll listen. I can't talk to my dad, and I want my kids to talk to me." Roger, 15

PERSONAL GROWTH

Gary says, "Tyrone was 14 years old when his teacher came to me about a problem. Tyrone had been severely depressed. He didn't have many friends, he was doing poorly in school, and there were troubles at home. At school, Tyrone kept to himself; at home, he spent most of his time watching TV or listening to the radio. Sometimes he wondered if it was worth it to go on living.

"I worked with Tyrone for two years. During that time, we did many things together, but mostly we got Tyrone involved in things that made him feel good about himself. One day a week he went to an elementary school and helped kindergarten children learn their colors and numbers. He got a dog and trained him to do tricks, and he learned to play the piano. Gradually Tyrone came out of his depression and started feeling happy to be alive. He made friends, graduated from high school, and got a job."

There was a lot wrong with Tyrone's life when he first met Gary, the most important being his self-concept. Tyrone didn't see himself as a useful and valuable person. Before he could change his self-concept, he had to start doing things that were useful and valuable. He had to experience personal growth and realize that he was worthwhile.

Many young people with LD develop a poor self-concept. This can happen for many reasons. Perhaps they have a hard time in school, or they think that having LD means that they are stupid, or they have trouble making friends. Any and all of these things can affect your self-concept. Fortunately, you can improve a poor self-concept. *If you do things that are useful and valuable, you will feel better about yourself.* We have seen this happen many times with teenagers we know.

People naturally want to be active. Have you ever watched a toddler? Unless the child is very tired, he or she is on the move all the time, touching, feeling, and tasting everything within reach. Do you know any elderly people? The healthy, happy ones stay active. They don't just sit around all day. When you turn on the TV, you turn off your brain. Maybe you don't feel like doing anything else, and maybe that's because you don't feel useful and valuable. Want to make a change? Want to feel good about yourself? Then try the following ideas for achieving personal growth and improving your self-concept. Some may seem hard; some may seem scary; but we promise that the effort will be worth it.

Dare to Do Something New

Tyrone was terrified the first time he went to the kindergarten class to help the kids. He didn't know what to expect, he didn't think the kids would like him, and he didn't believe he could help them. He wished he could change his mind and not go at all. He wanted to stay in his own class, even though he wasn't happy there.

Many unhappy people stay unhappy because they are afraid to try new things. If you don't take risks, you don't grow, and nothing ever changes in your life. We're not talking about unhealthy or dangerous risks like doing drugs or riding your skateboard down the freeway. We're talking about trying new things that will help you to grow. Maybe you're embarrassed to try them or you're afraid that you won't be any good. Maybe your usual response to anything new is "I don't have the energy" or "That sounds boring." Take a deep breath and jump into a new experience. It may turn out great—or it may bomb. Either way, you will grow personally because you took a risk and tried something new.

Volunteer.

There are many opportunities available to volunteer for good causes. There may be a homeless shelter that needs help serving or distributing food. A home for the elderly may need young people to keep lonely elderly people company. Perhaps there is a politician or political issue that you want to support. Check with your parents before you volunteer so they can make sure that the organization is reputable and the place is safe.

Learn a skill.

Is there a musical instrument you have always wanted to play? Would you like to know how to juggle? Do magic tricks? Play chess? Build something? Paint? Think about people who are experts in the skills you want to learn and ask them for help. What's the worst thing that can happen? They will say "no." More likely, they will say "yes."

Try some self-help or self-improvement.

Are you shy? Too loud? Do you have trouble thinking of things to say when you are with other people your age? Are you disorganized? Are you always late? There are groups and books to help people with all of these problems and more. Ask your school counselor for recommendations. Ask your local YMCA or YWCA, your church or synagogue about self-help groups. Visit your library and get help finding books on the subject you are interested in. If it's hard for you to read, ask the librarian for talking books. If there are no talking books, check out the regular books you want, then ask an adult to read them to you or tape record readings for you.

Develop a hobby.

Do you enjoy collecting baseball cards, stamps, or coins? Do you like making models? Are you into sewing or cooking? Whatever your interest is, make it your hobby. Whenever you have free time, work on your hobby instead of watching TV. This can also be a good way to meet people with similar interests.

And now for something completely different . . .

Have you ever been to an opera, ballet, symphony, or play? "Never!" you say. "That would be boring!" But how do you know until you try? Parks and recreation centers, cities, and shopping centers often sponsor free music and theater events. Ask your teacher or parents to help you find out when and where they will be, or look in your local newspaper. While you're at it, check out arts and crafts fairs, art exhibits, science fairs, and library activities. Are there hiking and bike trails in your community? Nature centers? Garden tours? Historic houses that are open to the public? As we write these words, we hear the music of a band playing in the park just outside our window. The music sounds wonderful, and there are many people sitting on the ground enjoying picnics while they listen. So go ahead and try something completely different.

Take On a New Responsibility

When Tyrone was working with the kindergarten children, he always made sure to show up on time. He was patient with the children and carefully did the tasks and assignments the teacher gave him. He took on the responsibility of working with the children, and he did a good job. The kids looked up to him and the teacher praised his work and his attitude. Tyrone started to feel good about himself. He had never thought of himself as a responsible person before, but he did now.

Taking on a new responsibility can be scary. What if you mess up? People will think you're a failure! On the other hand, what if you do a great job? People may give you even more responsibility! You may decide that you don't want more responsibility, and you may try to avoid it or get out of it. This is not a good choice for two reasons. First, you can't avoid responsibility forever, not if you plan to live on your own someday. And second, you will miss out on the rewards that come with responsibility: more freedom, respect, personal growth, and a positive self-concept.

Maybe you want to have more responsibility, but your parents and teachers don't trust you. Is it because of things you have done in the past? Is it because you don't act very responsible most of the time? If you want to be treated like a responsible person, you'll need to practice the three I's: Initiation, Invention, and Intervention.

Initiation.

To initiate something means to begin it. If you know that you are supposed to start dinner, set the table, vacuum the house, or some other chore, do it before you have to be reminded. Start working on your homework before your parents tell you. At school, be prepared for your classes.

Invention.

To invent something means to create it. You can invent your own responsibilities. Take over caring for the family pet, make a budget for your allowance, or offer to wash the car every Saturday morning. At school, you might volunteer to take attendance, collect materials at the end of a class period, or clean chalkboards between classes. What else needs to be done at home or at school? What other responsibilities can you invent for yourself?

IMPORTANT

If you invent a responsibility, you must follow through to prove that you are a responsible person. If you don't follow through, this will prove that you are not a responsible person. Don't make empty promises.

Intervention.

To intervene means to step in and get involved. Responsible people intervene when people need help and problems need solving. They don't just ignore them. For example, you see a teacher carrying too many books. Suddenly she drops some of them. Do you stop and help, or laugh and walk away? Or you notice your younger brother crying because he has lost a favorite toy. Do you look for it or tell him to shut up and grow up? You might get teased for helping at school and you might not get any thanks from your brother, even if you do find his toy. But intervention is still a good way to show that you are a responsible and caring person.

HEALTHY LIVING

People who feel good about themselves take care of their bodies so they can enjoy life for as long as possible. People who don't feel good about themselves may develop unhealthy habits such as eating a lot of junk food, avoiding exercise, and using alcohol and drugs. If you already have a poor self-concept, unhealthy habits will make it worse.

Healthy living can strengthen your self-concept. It also affects your learning and your emotions. Poor nutrition, lack of exercise, and the use of alcohol and drugs make it hard to learn new skills and ideas. They may make you feel depressed or useless. This chapter offers suggestions for changing bad habits into healthy habits.

Nutrition Know-How

Nevil was very sensitive to teasing. Whenever he felt sad or upset, he ate sweets—candy, donuts, cookies, ice cream. Eating seemed to cover up his unhappy feelings. Because of his poor eating habits, Nevil gained a lot of weight. When the other students started teasing him for getting fat, he felt even worse and ate even more. Nevil became extremely overweight. Finally he started seeing a counselor who helped him to understand that overeating wasn't the way to solve his problems.

Lisa believed that losing weight would make her more attractive. She wasn't overweight, but she thought she was. She bought some diet pills at the drugstore, ate very little for the next several days, and lost ten pounds. But she wanted to lose more, so she kept taking the pills and eating almost nothing. Eventually she became so thin that her parents took her to the hospital, where it was found that Lisa had a condition called anorexia. She had nearly starved herself to death.

Both Nevil and Lisa had eating disorders, and they needed professional help. If you think you might have an eating disorder, please talk to your parents, your school counselor, a teacher, or another adult you trust, and do it soon.

Most young people don't have eating disorders, but they may have unhealthy eating habits. Do you eat a lot of junk food, fast food, and sweets? They are easy to get, easy to eat, and they taste good, but they are not good for you. Do you drink a lot of coffee, tea, or soft drinks with caffeine? They can make you restless and irritable and keep you from getting to sleep at night. Do you skip breakfast and lunch, then eat too much at dinner? You may have trouble concentrating because you don't eat regular meals.

Following are three ways to improve your eating habits.

Plan a healthful diet.

Do you know what foods are good for you? Do you know how much Vitamin C a teenager needs each day? Do you know what a balanced meal includes? If you can't answer these questions—and if you want to follow a healthier diet—make an appointment with your school nurse and ask for help in planning a healthful diet. If your school doesn't have a nurse, ask for help at a health clinic, the county health department, or your family physician's office. Many communities also have health fairs where nutrition information is available free of charge. Visit your library and look for books, articles, and pamphlets on diet and nutrition.

Avoid crash diets and diet pills.

Do you think you need to lose weight? First, check with a nurse or a doctor. You may discover that your current weight is just right for your age, size, and body type. If you decide to go on a diet, get advice from your nurse or doctor. Don't start a crash diet of your own or take diet pills. You may lose a lot of weight quickly, but you will almost certainly gain it back. This yo-yo effect—your weight goes down, then up, then down, then up again—is hard on your body and especially your heart.

Learn to cook.

Take a cooking class at school or ask someone who knows how to cook to teach you the basics. Then you will be able to prepare your own healthful meals and snacks. When you know how to cook, you will become more aware of what goes into the foods you eat. You will start reading the labels on packaged foods, and you will discover that many are full of chemicals. Why would you want to eat chemicals when you can have fresh, delicious food you fix yourself?

Exercise Expertise

"I hate exercise."

Have you ever said those words? True, it's no fun to run a mile in P.E. class or do a hundred push-ups and sit-ups. Almost nobody enjoys that kind of exercise, but there are other kinds that can be a lot of fun. One of the best is called aerobic exercise. The goal of aerobic exercise is to increase your heart rate to a certain range and keep it there for 20 to 45 minutes. People who do this three to four times a week tend to live longer, feel better, and sleep better than people who don't.

You may think that aerobic exercise means running, jogging, or going to classes where people jump around to loud music, but those are only a few types of aerobic exercise. Following are several more. Which ones sound like fun to you?

- walking fast
- riding a bicycle
- roller skating
- jumping rope
- jumping on a trampoline
- cross-country skiing

- swimming
- working out on exercise equipment like rowing machines, stair machines, or ski machines

How can you tell if you are getting aerobic exercise? Take your pulse for six seconds. If your heart beats from 12 to 17 times in 6 seconds, you are getting aerobic exercise. If your heart beats more than 17 times, you may be exercising too hard; if your heart beats fewer than 12 times, you may need to exercise a little harder. To get the maximum benefits from aerobic exercise, you want to stay in the range of 12 to 17 heartbeats in 6 seconds, or 120 to 170 beats per minute, for 20 to 45 minutes.

Before starting any exercise program, check with your doctor. This is especially important if you have done little or no exercise in the past.

EXERCISE TIPS TO HELP YOU SUCCEED

1. Exercise with a friend; it's more fun than doing it alone, and you can motivate each other. If one of you says, "Oh, not today, I feel too tired and lazy," the other can say, "Let's go!"

2. If you have to exercise alone, listen to music or go someplace interesting. Running around a track can be boring, so try running around your neighborhood or down a nature path and enjoy being outdoors while you exercise.

3. Vary your exercise; don't do the same thing every time. You might jump rope one day and go in-line skating another day.

4. Don't overdo it. If you are just starting an exercise program, take it easy. If you try to exercise every day for 45 minutes, you will get very tired and sore and you will probably quit. Start slowly and gradually increase the amount of exercise and the length of time.

5. Always stretch your muscles for 10 to 15 minutes before you exercise and 10 to 15 minutes after you finish. This prevents you from injuring yourself and from getting tight, sore muscles.

Alcohol and Drugs

We have done some research into alcohol, drugs, and students with LD, and our research has shown that students with LD have more problems with alcohol and drugs than other students. We think this happens because students with LD tend to be more unhappy in school. They feel like they don't fit in, so they use alcohol and drugs to cover up sad and lonely feelings, to increase their self-confidence, and to fit in with other students. But alcohol and drugs don't solve problems, they cause problems. When the effects wear off, you still have LD. You are less confident than you were before, you feel more sad and lonely, and you may be in trouble for using the alcohol or drugs.

Alcohol and drugs change our brain chemistry and make us think and feel things that aren't true. See for yourself. Go to a party sometime and stay straight—don't use any alcohol or drugs. Watch the people who are using. Are they as funny, smart, interesting, and attractive as they think they are? Or do they look and act really stupid?

Students with LD may already have a hard time learning in school. Using alcohol and drugs makes it even harder. Following are a few examples of what we mean.

- Alcohol impairs your judgment and reasoning and distorts your emotions. It can also give you a terrible hangover. How can you learn when your head is pounding and you feel like throwing up?

- Marijuana (also called "pot" or "weed") affects your short-term memory. Regular use of marijuana makes you feel like sitting around and not doing much of anything.

- Inhalants such as glue, gasoline, and aerosols can cause brain, kidney, liver, and heart damage—even death.

- Cocaine, crack cocaine, and crank (methamphetamine or "speed") distort your judgment, reasoning, and emotions. They are also highly addictive.

You have heard the "just say no" campaigns. You may have taken part in a D.A.R.E. program to keep young people off of drugs. You may already know a lot about alcohol and drugs—more than we can tell you here. But you may not have known that students with LD have more problems with alcohol and drugs than other students. We hope that you will see this as one more reason not to use alcohol and drugs.

Another drug we want to mention briefly is nicotine, the highly addictive drug found in tobacco products. We don't have to tell you about the serious diseases caused by the use of tobacco products. If you smoke cigarettes and you aren't too worried about what will happen 30 years from now, then consider the money you are spending, your bad breath, and the horrible smell on your clothes. Also think about this: There is new evidence that second-hand smoke causes cancer and heart disease. In other words, smoking isn't just harmful to your health. It's harmful to the health of the people you smoke around.

If you think you may have a problem with alcohol or drugs, or if you just want help staying away from drugs, contact your school counselor or another adult you trust. Or look in the Yellow Pages under "Alcoholism Information and Treatment Centers." You will find the names of many places that help people with alcohol and drug problems. Some offer free and confidential counseling.

FOR MORE INFORMATION

Here are organizations you can write to or call for more information about alcohol and drugs. Notice that some have toll-free 800 numbers.

America's PRIDE Program
National Parents' Resource Institute for Drug Education
50 Hurt Plaza, Suite 210
Atlanta, GA 30303
(404) 577-4500

American Council for Drug Education
204 Monroe Street, Suite 110
Rockville, MD 20850
(800) 488-DRUG (that's 800-488-3784)

"Just Say No" Clubs
1777 North California Boulevard, Suite 210
Walnut Creek, CA 94596
(800) 258-2766
If you are in the 415 area code, call 939-6666

The National Clearinghouse for Alcohol
and Drug Information
P.O. Box 2345
Rockville, MD 20852
(800) 729-6686

National Crime Prevention Council
DARE Program
1700 K Street NW, Second Floor
Washington, DC 20006
(202) 466-6272

Students Against Driving Drunk (SADD)
P.O. Box 800
Marlboro, MA 01752
(508) 481-3568

Students To Offset Peer Pressure (STOPP)
P.O. Box 103
Hudson, NH 03051-0103
(603) 889-8163

Toll-free hotlines:
(800) 662-HELP (that's 800-662-4357)
(800) COCAINE (that's 800-262-2463)

BEING A GOOD CITIZEN

Have you noticed that people today spend a lot of time talking about their rights? Some teenagers think that their right to freedom of speech means they can say anything, anytime, anywhere, to anyone they please—even if their words hurt other people. Some teenagers think it is their right to buy any music or see any movie they choose. Some believe it is their right to stay out as long as they like or play their music as loud as they want to hear it. Others claim it is their right to drink alcohol or smoke cigarettes, since they own their bodies and can do with them whatever they please.

We're glad we live in a country where citizens have so many rights. But we're concerned that so many teenagers and adults are demanding their rights without accepting the responsibilities that go along with them. People who exercise their rights without thinking about how their behavior affects others are selfish and immature. In Chapter 2, we wrote about the "three R's" of rights, responsibilities, and respect. Remember that they always go together.

Rhoda says, "Stella was a 13-year-old who came to my office one day after school. She told me that some kids had ganged up on her in the lunch room and called her names. When a teacher heard what was happening, he told the kids to go to the counselor's office. The kids told the teacher that they could say whatever they wanted because of their right to free speech.

"Stella asked me, 'Do people have the right to say whatever they want? Even if it hurts someone else?' I answered, 'People in this country can say whatever they want. But most people try not to abuse their right to free speech. Those boys who called you names were abusing their right. They aren't mature enough to understand the responsibilities that go along with their rights.'"

Good citizens don't abuse their rights. They are aware of times when exercising their rights might harm someone else, and they make decisions that are respectful of other people. For example:

- People of legal age have the right to smoke cigarettes. Good citizens make sure that their smoking doesn't bother anyone else.

- People have the right to get together in a crowd. Good citizens don't disturb the peace or destroy property.

- People who are licensed have the right to drive a car. Good citizens obey the traffic laws and don't use their cars to endanger other people.

When you talk about your rights, do you remember your responsibilities? Do you respect the rights and needs of other people?

Four Ways to Be a Good Citizen: Tips for Younger Teenagers

You may think that being a good citizen just means paying your taxes and voting in elections. But what if you don't have to pay taxes and you're too young to vote? You can still be a good citizen.

1. Treat other people with respect.

Be polite to other students in the hallway or cafeteria. Don't say or do things that will hurt other people. This is how you want to be treated, and it is also how other people want to be treated. Try to put yourself in their place and imagine how they would feel if you said or did something careless or hurtful.

There are some people who go out of their way to be mean to teenagers with LD. They make fun of them for attending special classes, or they tease them and call them names. If other students are treating you badly, you may think this gives you the right to do the same to them. Instead, try treating them with respect. You might say something like, "How would you feel if I called you names? You wouldn't like it, and neither do I." They might think about how they would feel, and sometimes—but not always—they will stop being mean.

Treat your parents and teachers with respect. When they are kind to you, return their kindness. When they take time to help you, thank them and show how much you appreciate their help and support.

2. Respect other people's property.

Some teenagers think that anything that belongs to their parents, brothers, or sisters also belongs to them. They think they have a right to borrow whatever they want without asking. How would you feel if you went to your closet and found that someone had borrowed your favorite shirt? Or you went to your tool box and found that someone had borrowed your tools? Always ask first. If someone says, "No, you can't borrow my shirt" or "No, you can't borrow my tools," listen and respect his or her wishes.

Sometimes teenagers get together and destroy other people's property. We know a young couple who worked hard, saved their money, and bought a house. The house was old and needed a lot of work, but our friends fixed it up. They spent almost a year painting the house, planting grass, and building a fence around the yard. By the time they were finished, the house looked great. Not long after, on a night when our friends were away, a group of teenagers sprayed black paint all over their fence and drove a car across their yard. A neighbor called the police, but when they arrived the teenagers were gone. It took our friends several months to repair the damage to their fence and yard.

If just one of the teenagers had stopped to think, "How will these people feel?", that might have been enough to prevent the damage. Sometimes teenagers do things in a group that they would never do by themselves. Good citizens do the right thing, even if it means going against the group. Don't let other people talk you into actions or behaviors you know are wrong.

3. Protect the environment.

Most teenagers are aware that our environment is in trouble. It can be discouraging to hear all the news reports about the environment. The rain forest and the ozone layer are being destroyed. Lakes and rivers are dying. The air is polluted. These are not cheerful topics. Sometimes things seem so bad that you feel hopeless and powerless to make a difference.

We believe that everyone can work to protect the environment. There are hundreds of things you can do alone and with your friends. Don't litter, and pick up other people's litter. Ride your bike or the bus instead of driving a car. Recycle, stop using aerosol sprays, and plant a tree. Work with a group to clean up a stream or a lakeshore. Every responsible action or decision makes a difference. What are you doing today to protect the environment, and what else can you do tomorrow?

4. Take responsibility for your own behavior.

Some teenagers like to blame other people when things go wrong. Do any of the following sound familiar?

"So I failed my math test. It's my mom's fault. She said she would help me study and she didn't."

"I'm bored. It's because my friends are boring."

"Late to school again! It's my dad's fault. He was supposed to wake me up this morning."

"I didn't mean to crash the car. My friends were talking too loud. I got distracted."

"Breaking that window wasn't my idea. My friends made me do it."

You are responsible for your own behavior—no exceptions. If you fail a test, it's up to you to do better next time. Ask the teacher for help. If you're bored, don't depend on others to entertain you. Go to the library and check out some books, build a model airplane, volunteer at a hospital or a shelter for homeless people. If you're always late to school, that's your problem. Get an alarm clock and get yourself up in time for school. Who do you think will wake you up when you're on your own and you have to go to work?

Four More Ways to Be a Good Citizen: Tips for Older Teenagers

The four tips for younger teenagers are meant for you, too. But because you have special rights that younger teenagers don't have, you also have special responsibilities.

1. Be a safe driver.

If you have the right to drive, you also have responsibilities that go along with driving.* Many teenagers think that driving a car makes them powerful. They think that driving fast makes them look cool to their friends. If you can't drive safely, you're not mature enough to drive. Wait until you are.

2. Be an involved citizen.

Although you can't vote in political elections until you are 18, you can get involved in local, state, and national politics at any age. Learn as much as you can about the political process. Attend a school board meeting or a city council meeting. If possible, visit your state capitol and watch the legislature at work. Find out how laws are written and passed. Visit your representative's office, ask questions, and express any concerns you might have. If you have a concern about a community issue, call the mayor or a city council member and share your concern.

Gary says, "The grass in one of our city parks was brown and dying. A young woman named Cynthia who went to the park every day noticed the problem. Several weeks passed and the grass continued to die; even some of the trees were starting to look bad. Finally Cynthia decided to do something about it. She called the mayor's office and explained what was happening to the park. The mayor was surprised; he hadn't heard about the problem. He drove to the park and saw the damage for himself. When he did some checking, he discovered a broken water pump that should have been repaired months before. The mayor ordered that the pump be repaired immediately. Within a few days, the grass was green again."

---

* Many of these responsibilities are described in Chapter 8.

MAKING A DIFFERENCE

If you enjoy reading about young people who are making a difference, here are three books you won't want to miss.

- *The Kid's Guide to Social Action* by Barbara A. Lewis. Free Spirit Publishing Inc., 1991. This book includes many stories about young people. It also explains how you can get involved and make a difference.

- *Kids with Courage* by Barbara A. Lewis. Free Spirit Publishing Inc., 1992. Eighteen exciting stories about young people who are fighting crime, working to save the environment, and more.

- *150 Ways Teens Can Make a Difference: A Handbook for Action* by Marian Salzman, Teresa Reisgies, and Thousands of Teenage Contributors. Peterson's Guides, 1991. Organizations, people to contact, and first-person experiences.

3. Keep up with the news.

Read the newspaper and watch the local news on TV to stay informed about events in your community, state, country, and the world. Try to learn something about other people everywhere, and help out in whatever way you can. For example, if you hear that some people in your community need warm clothes for the winter, ask your parents if you can donate clothes you no longer wear. Ask if they have any clothes to donate. If you hear that people are starving, volunteer to help an organization that works to feed starving people.

4. Register to vote, and vote whenever you can.

When you turn 18, you may register to vote. In some states, you may do this when you register your car at the State Department of Motor Vehicles; in other states, you may register at the voting place on election day. The right to vote is one of the most important rights you will ever have. Along with this right comes the responsibility to learn about the people who are running for office. Listen to their speeches to find out where they stand on the issues, then vote for the candidates you believe will do the best job. Vote in every election, local and national, and don't skip the primaries, since their outcomes determine the candidates for the general elections.

CONTINUING YOUR EDUCATION

Before long, you will graduate from high school. Graduation is an important event in the lives of most teenagers—the beginning of adulthood and independence, and the end of childhood and dependence. However, it shouldn't be the end of your education. We hope that you'll keep learning for the rest of your life. You may decide to continue your formal education at a vocational school, a community or junior college, or a four-year college or university. But even if you choose to start working full-time immediately after graduation, there are many ways to continue your informal education. Following are three suggestions for you to consider.*

Take a Class

"No more school!"

If that's what you're thinking, relax. There are classes you can take for fun, to satisfy your curiosity, to pursue an interest, or to

_____

* The ideas for personal growth presented in Chapter 11 are also excellent ways to continue your informal education.

develop a skill. For example, would you like to learn how to dance? Bake bread? Take pictures? Draw or paint? Train your dog? Cook Italian food? Change the oil in your car? Plant a garden? Speak Spanish? Sew your own clothes? Act in a play? Many towns and cities offer community education classes. They are usually taught in the evenings at local schools or park buildings and anyone can take them. For most of these classes, there are no requirements, tests, or grades.

If school has been a struggle for you, the thought of taking more classes may be scary. You may think that you can't succeed at anything. Give yourself a chance and sign up for a class that sounds interesting to you. If you show up for class, you will succeed, and you may discover talents and abilities you never knew you had. Following are two more reasons to take a class:

- You will meet new people. Since you signed up for the same class, you already have something in common.

- The people in the class will probably have a wide range of abilities. They may be different ages and come from different backgrounds. Everybody will have the same opportunity to learn, and nobody will be labeled "LD" or "not LD." If you have been teased in the past because you have LD, it will be a big relief to be treated like everyone else.

Join a Club or Organization

Every Wednesday our local newspaper publishes a list of clubs and organizations. There are bicycle clubs, hiking clubs, self-help groups, support groups, exercise clubs, garden clubs, writers' groups, actors' groups, bird-watchers' groups, and many more. Find out if and when your local paper publishes this kind of list. Choose a club or organization that looks interesting, call the telephone number listed in the paper, and request more information. When you find a club or organization you would like to get involved in, ask a friend or parent to accompany you until you feel comfortable going alone.

We encourage you to join the Learning Disabilities Association (LDA). This national organization, with active state and local chapters, provides information and support for people with LD and their families. To find out more, write or call:

Learning Disabilities Association
4156 Library Road
Pittsburgh, PA 15234
(412) 341-1515

Three more organizations for people with LD are:

Marin Puzzle People
1368 Lincoln Avenue
Suite 105
San Rafael, CA 94701
(415) 383-8763

The National Center for Learning Disabilities, Inc.
99 Park Avenue
New York, NY 10016
(212) 687-7211

National Network of Learning Disabled Adults
808 North 82nd Street
Suite F-2
Scottsdale, AZ 85257
(602) 941-5112.

Form a Group

You probably know other teenagers with LD who will soon be graduating from high school. Ask if they would like to get together on a regular basis—for example, once a month. There is power in numbers. A group of adults with LD can think of many ways to help one another and reach out to young people and children with LD. If you are unsure about how to organize such a group, ask a teacher or your parents to help you get started.

BEING THE BEST YOU CAN BE

Bill was in the LD program all through high school because he had trouble reading. He wanted to be an auto mechanic, so after he graduated he got a job as an assistant at a repair shop. At first he was given all the jobs that nobody else wanted to do, but he came to work on time every day, did his job, and was friendly to the customers and the other employees. Eventually he was promoted to mechanic and then to shop supervisor. Bill still has LD, and he still doesn't read very well, but Bill is a successful person.

Ana completed seven years of college before becoming a teacher and a school counselor. Because of her LD, college was very difficult for her, but she worked hard and refused to give up. Like Bill, Ana is a successful person who happens to have LD.

LD is often called an invisible handicap. Unlike the inability to walk, see, or hear, LD isn't obvious except in certain learning situations. Because LD is invisible, many people who have LD feel misunderstood by others. They come to believe that words like "stupid," "lazy," and "dumb" apply to them. Fortunately, more people are learning about LD, and the more they learn, the less misunderstanding there will be. Many teachers and counselors today have been specially trained to work with students who have LD. They know about the different kinds of LD, and they are helping students with LD learn in ways that are right for them. Also, there are laws that guarantee certain rights to people with LD. These laws can help and protect you.

Having LD may make it difficult for you to achieve, but it doesn't make it impossible. You can be a success in many ways: in a job, in living on your own, in relationships with others, even in school. How successful can you be? That depends more on the kind of person you are than on the kind of LD you have. If you are a responsible, dependable person who works hard and gets along with others, you will probably do well in life even if you have serious learning differences. If you aren't responsible and dependable, you probably won't get what you want in life even if your learning differences are very minor.

You can't change the fact that you have LD. There is no magic cure for your learning differences. But you can decide for yourself what kind of person you are and will be. In this book, we have given you many suggestions for being your best, and we hope you will try them. They have helped other teenagers with LD and they can help you, too.

Some people with LD have become enormously successful and even famous. For example:

- Nelson Rockefeller had a severe reading problem. He became governor of New York and vice president of the United States.

- Ann Bancroft was held back in school because she had trouble learning to read. She became the first woman to reach the North Pole.

- Bruce Jenner and Greg Louganis had reading problems in school; Greg also had a speech problem. Both went on to win gold medals in the Olympics.

- When Thomas Edison was a boy, people thought he was retarded. He became one of America's most famous inventors.

- Susan Hampshire had trouble paying attention in school. She has won three Emmy Awards for acting on TV.

- If you go to movies, then you have heard of Tom Cruise, Goldie Hawn, Cher, and Whoopi Goldberg. All four are famous and successful actors, and they all have LD.

It's true that most people with LD don't become famous—but neither do most people without LD. What's important is for you to be your best. Make that your goal and you will succeed.

WHEN YOU'RE READY FOR MORE

Now that you have read *The Survival Guide for Teenagers with LD*, we hope you will continue to learn about LD. Following is one book we recommend. Check your library for other books and articles you may want to read.

- *Succeeding Against the Odds: Strategies and Insights from the Learning Disabled* by Sally L. Smith. Jeremy P. Tarcher, 1991. Practical techniques and inspiring stories help you learn how to reach your full potential and succeed in life.

INDEX

Trampolines, and
exercise, 158
Transportation
bus, 115-118
car, 121-126
independent, 115-
126
long-distance, 119-
121
to special services,
28
Travel, long-distance,
119-121
making connections,
120
money needed, 120-
121
and strangers, 121
Trust, earning
parents', 111

U

Universities. *See*
Colleges/universities
Utilities, and apart-
ment rental, 108-109

V

Vocational rehabilita-
tion agency, state
and career choice,
90, 94-95
Vocational schools.
See Trade/vocational
schools
Volunteer work
and job skill develop-
ment, 48-49, 80
and personal growth,
149
Voting, 173

W

WAIS. *See* Wechsler
Intelligence Test for
Adults (WAIS)
Walker, Alice, on
friendship, 134
Walking, as exercise,
158
Washington, George,
on friendship, 134
Weaknesses, and
assertiveness, 43-44
Wechsler Intelligence
Test for Adults
(WAIS), 13
Wechsler Intelligence
Test for Children
(WISC), 13
*What Teenagers Want
to Know about Sex*
(Masland), 142
*The What's Happening
to My Body Book for
Boys* (Madaras), 141
*The What's Happening
to My Body Book for
Girls* (Madaras), 142
Wide Range
Achievement Test
(WRAT), 13
Wilkes, Donald L., on
job hunting, 76
WISC. *See* Wechsler
Intelligence Test for
Children (WISC)
Woodcock Reading
Master Test, 13
Words, understanding
meaning of, 8
WRAT. *See* Wide
Range Achievement
Test (WRAT)

Y

Yard work, 69-70
YMCA
baby-sitting pro-
grams, 68, 69
and personal growth,
150
YWCA
baby-sitting
programs, 68
and personal growth,
150

MORE BOOKS FROM FREE SPIRIT

Bringing Up Parents:
The Teenager's Handbook
by Alex J. Packer, Ph.D.

Straight talk and specific suggestions on how teens can take the initiative to resolve conflicts with parents, improve family relationships, earn trust, accept responsibility, and help create a healthier, happier home environment. Ages 13 and up.

176 pp; illus; s/c; 7 1/4" x 9 1/4"
ISBN 0-915793-48-2; $12.95

Making the Most of Today:
Daily Readings for Young People on
Self-Awareness, Creativity, and Self-Esteem
by Pamela Espeland and Rosemary Wallner

Daily readings for all kids who want to know themselves better, be more creative, and feel more confident. Ages 11 and up.

392 pp; s/c; 4" x 7"
ISBN 0-915793-33-4; $8.95

Kids with Courage:
True Stories about Young People Making a Difference
by Barbara A. Lewis

Exciting true accounts of kids taking social action, fighting crime, working to save the environment, and performing heroic acts. Ages 11 and up.

160 pp; illus; s/c; 6" x 9"
ISBN 0-915793-39-3; $10.95

School Power:
Strategies for Succeeding in School
by Jeanne Shay Schumm, Ph.D.
and Marguerite Radencich, Ph.D.

Covers getting organized, taking notes, studying smarter, writing better, following directions, handling homework, managing long-term assignments, and more. Ages 11 and up.

144 pp; s/c; B&W photos; 8 1/2" x 11"
ISBN 0-915793-42-3; $11.95

To place an order or to request a free SELF-HELP FOR KIDS® catalog,
write or call:

Free Spirit Publishing Inc.
400 First Avenue North, Suite 616
Minneapolis, MN 55401-1730
toll-free (800) 735-7323
local (612) 338-2068